Physical Characteristics of the Doberman Pinscher

(from the American Kennel Club breed standard)

Tail: Docked at approximately second joint, appears to be a continuation of the spine, and is carried only slightly above the horizontal when the dog is alert.

Hindquarters: The angulation of the hindquarters balances that of the forequarters. Upper shanks at right angles to the hip bones, are long, wide, and well muscled on both sides of thigh, with clearly defined stifles. Upper and lower shanks are of equal length.

Coat: Smooth-haired, short, hard, thick and close lying.

Color and Markings: Allowed Colors: Black, red, blue, and fawn (Isabella). Markings: Rust, sharply defined, appearing above each eye and on muzzle, throat and forechest, on all legs and feet, and below tail.

Height: Dogs 26 to 28 inches, ideal about 27.5 inches; Bitches 24 to 26 inches, ideal about 25.5 inches.

Doberman Pinscher

by Lou-Ann Cloidt

Contents

KENNEL CLUB BOOKS: **DOBERMAN PINSCHER**

ISBN: 1-59378-230-6

Kennel Club Books, Inc., 308 Main Street, Allenhurst, NJ 07711 USA
Cover Design Patented: US 6,435,559 B2 • Printed in South Korea

Photos by Michael Trafford with additional photos by:
Norvia Behling, Carolina Biological Supply, Kent and Donna Dannen, Doskocil, Isabelle Français, James Hayden-Yoav, James R. Hayden, RBP, Carol Ann Johnson, Bill Jonas, Dwight R. Kuhn, Dr. Dennis Kunkel, Mikki Pet Products, Phototake, Jean Claude Revy, Dr. Andrew Spielman, Nikki Sussman, Karen J. Taylor and C. James Webb.

Illustrations by Renée Low and Patricia Peters.

The publisher wishes to thank Homike Kennels, Kristiina Luukkanen, Elaine and Steve Rome (Purroma Kennels), Laura Spear, Denise Thomas, Denine Voorls and the rest of the owners of Doberman Pinschers featured in this book.

Devised as a specialized guard dog, the Doberman Pinscher must be fearless and biddable, always making his master his first priority.

To serve man as a guard dog and protector, the Doberman Pinscher possesses a powerful frame, well muscled and agile.

HISTORY OF THE DOBERMAN PINSCHER

There are several hundred breeds of dog that have complicated ancestries. The "true" origin of many breeds is surrounded by speculation and uncertainty, and the Doberman Pinscher is no exception. This medium-sized working breed is the epitômé of strength, agility and endurance. The breed's original purpose was two-fold. First, it was originally developed to control vermin. Second, and most important, its purpose was to protect man as a specialized guard dog. From the very beginning, the Doberman Pinscher's reputation for strength of character and its influence as an imposing figure were widely recognized and valued. The breed was first developed as a working dog to serve mankind, and it continues to hold that purpose today.

In comparison with other breeds, the Doberman Pinscher is of relatively recent vintage. Karl Friedrick Louis Dobermann, born in 1834 in Apolda, Germany, is widely accepted as the developer of the breed that originated around 1890 in Apolda, in Thueringen, Germany. The breed was originally referred to as Dobermann's Dog. "Pinscher," which translates to "terrier" in German, was later added to its name (in the United Kingdom, the breed is known simply as the Dobermann). The breed has always been a working animal, and the word "pinscher" reflects the original purpose of vermin control.

Louis Dobermann's background is as much of an uncertainty as the breed that carries his name. Dobermann was said to have held several different occupations before his death in 1893. He was a tax collector, nightwatchman, meat cutter, dog catcher and manager of the animal shelter in his area. Regardless of his place of employment, his skills as a breeder were recognized despite his modest education. His intentions were to set out and create a medium- to large-sized working dog that would protect him during his travels throughout the day. Although Dobermann kept no breeding records, it was not long before he was successful with his attempts.

Its German brethren in black and tan, the Rottweiler contributed its unique coloration and some of its brawn to the Doberman Pinscher.

"SCHNUPPS" ANYONE?

In the Germany of yesteryear, the Doberman Pinscher was also known as "Schnupps," which means police or soldier dogs.

Most agree that the Doberman Pinscher is a descendant of the Rottweiler, smooth-haired German Pinscher, Thueringian Shepherd and Great Dane. In the late 1800s, there were some indications that the breed was also crossed with the Greyhound, German Shorthaired Pointer and Manchester Terrier. The Doberman Pinscher absorbed many positive qualities from each of these breeds; all of them greatly contributed to its foundation. For example, the Manchester was said to give the breed a darker eye and improve the quality of the coat with its shortness and deep tan markings. The Greyhound likely contributed to the breed's sleekness, and the Rottweiler supplied the black-and-tan coloration.

During the 1800s, the city of Apolda was a flourishing trade center. A popular annual event

Some authorities claim that the German Shorthaired Pointer was used in the creation of the Doberman Pinscher, possibly contributing to the breed's intelligence and trainability.

was known as the "dog market." This festival took place each year on the seventh Sunday after Easter and featured a parade of dogs. The event attracted hundreds of spectators who crowded the streets to take part in the celebration. Participants enjoyed fine foods and refreshments but, most importantly, gathered anxiously to await the arrival of the dogs. Many local dog breeders arrived with their breeding stock for public sale. In those days, many of the dogs were mixed breeds. In all likelihood, Louis Dobermann proudly displayed his Doberman Pinschers at this annual event.

Early specimens of the breed were extremely heavy-set, with stocky, coarse heads. Like several other working breeds of the time, the Doberman Pinscher was developed primarily for protection. Early specimens were very different from the square, muscular, compactly built Doberman Pinschers bred today. Louis Dobermann, and many other breeders who followed him during that era, were concerned more with the breed's guard-dog qualities and characteristics than its conformation. Early examples of the breed in the 1900s continued to have coarse heads, poor fronts and short legs.

After Dobermann's death, several other breeders continued to improve and move forward with

Early crosses with the Manchester Terrier improved the quality of the Doberman Pinscher's sleek black-and-tan coat.

The German Pinscher is considered the most ancient of the three pinscher breeds. The Doberman is the largest, and the Miniature Pinscher is the smallest.

the breed's development. They included Otto Goeller, Goswin Tishler and Gustav Krumbholz. Goeller was one of the first breeders who started to refine the Doberman Pinscher from its thick-bodied appearance. He began concentrating more on elegance as an important breed quality.

DOBERMAN PINSCHERS IN THE UNITED STATES

The first Doberman Pinscher was imported to the United States by E. R. Salmann in 1898. Unfortunately, little information is available about Salmann or his dog. According to the AKC's (American Kennel Club) Stud Book, Doberman Intelectus (a black-and-tan) was the first dog listed in this book in 1908. This dog's sire was Doberman Bertel, a German import, and his dam was Doberman Hertha. Doberman Hertha earned her championship in 1912 and became the first recorded American champion. Ch. Doberman Dix was the first male and first American-bred champion. The Doberman Pinscher Club of America was founded in February 1921.

In the beginning, prior to the start of the war in Europe, the style of the American Doberman Pinscher was tremendously influenced by the breeders of German and Dutch heritage. By the late 1930s and early 1940s, many

THE DICTATOR STUD

Ch. Dictator of Glenhugel was one of the breed's most renowned stud dogs. He is remembered for passing along two distinctive traits: the first was his favorable temperament and the second was a cowlick at the "nape" of his neck. Dogs that have this cowlick are said to have the "mark of Dictator."

The early crossings with the swift and graceful Greyhound are indicated in some German breeding accounts.

influential dogs began to emerge. Ch. Westphalia's Rameses was one of these instrumental dogs. Rameses produced Ch. Dow's Illena of Marineland, who later produced 12 champions. This was quite an accomplishment for this time period. The record was broken first by Ch. Patton's Ponder of Torn, who sired 16 champions, and then by Ch. Brown's Dion, who sired 35 champions. The Doberman Pinschers of this time had low croups, short necks, long backs, light eyes, short heads and poor fronts. Some other leading producers from the early 1940s through the early 1960s were Ch. Alcor v. Millsdod, Ch. Dictator v. Glenhugel, Ch. Delegate v. Elbe and Ch. Steb's Top Skipper.

The American Doberman Pinscher is a stylish, elegant working dog with dramatically cropped ears.

DOBERMAN PINSCHERS IN PURPLE AND GOLD

The most prestigious show in America is surely the Westminster Kennel Club dog show, held each year in New York City. It is the longest running dog show in the world. The first Doberman Pinscher to claim the Best in Show trophy did so in 1939, Ch. Ferry v. Rauhfelsen of Giralda (owned by the famous Giralda Farms). In 1952 and 1953, Ch. Rancho Dobe's Storm (owned by Mr. and Mrs. Len Carey) did what few show dogs have ever accomplished by winning Westminster for two consecutive years. Over four decades later, in 1989, Ch. Royal Tudor's Wild As The Wind (owned by Richard and Carolyn Vida, Bethe Wilhite and Arthur and Susan Korp) took the honor as the last Doberman of the 20th century to claim this prestigious win.

Unfortunately, the early 1960s was also a period when the Doberman Pinscher received damaging public criticism. There were a few isolated incidents that would severely damage the breed's image for several years to come. A few cases of small children being attacked and killed by the breed quickly resulted in all Doberman Pinschers being labeled as vicious, man-eating dogs. The media quickly jumped on these incidents, and the breed's temperament was under strict scrutiny well into the late 1960s. It was not until the early 1970s

The Deutsche Dogge, as the Great Dane is known in Germany, is frequently identified as an early predecessor of the Doberman Pinscher.

that things finally settled down and the breed began to make a strong comeback in the U.S.

Women played a huge role in the style, direction and shaping of the American Doberman Pinscher. This was very different from Europe, where the breeders were, for the most part, male. In fact, as late as 1983, Margaret Bastable was the only woman in Germany that was licensed to judge Doberman Pinschers. Some of the top influential American female breeders include Peggy Adamson, Tess Hensler, Jane Kay and Joanna Walker—to name just a few.

THE DOBERMANN IN THE UNITED KINGDOM

Dobermanns were first imported to England in the mid-1920s, but their numbers were inconsequential. There were fewer than a dozen imported before the start of World War II. At first, the breed

Doberman Pinschers have a long history of police work. These dogs were shown in a police dog competition in Moscow, Russia at the turn of the 20th century.

had a limited following. One of the early imports that made a huge impact on the country was a bitch named Ossi v. Stresow. "Ossi" was owned by famous author and cooking expert Elizabeth Craig. The dog's popularity was enormous. Ossi was featured in *The Sunday Express* and nicknamed "The Most Romantic Dog in the World."

Unfortunately, the quality of early Dobermann imports to Great Britain was extremely poor. By today's show standards, they would be considered "pet quality" at best. Some of the first dogs imported to England possessed many of the same unfavorable characteristics as many of the early American dogs. For a working dog, the breed was not sound. They were poor movers, the result of weak fronts, shallow chests, bad feet and coarse outlines. Finding a decent-quality dog was nearly impossible. Furthermore, in the late 1930s and early 1940s, most of the top specimens found in Germany were not being made available to interested English parties. Therefore, the residents of the United Kingdom were forced to develop their own breeding programs and bloodlines from the limited stock that was made available. Four individuals that were responsible for this movement were Lionel Hamilton-Renwick, Fred and Julia Curnow and Peter Pitt-Milward.

The Curnows established the famous Tavey Kennels. The Tavey Kennels would become a big influence in the effort to breed better quality Dobermanns in England for several years to come. In 1948, the Dobermann Club was formed in the United Kingdom. Its name would later be changed to The Doberman Pinscher Club. Sir Noel Curtis-Bennet was the first president and Fred Curnow was the chairman. After moving to

Exhibits from abroad, as well as from England, arrived for the Crystal Palace show in London in 1933, organized by England's Kennel Club. The only German dog at the show was a Doberman Pinscher, shown here with famed writer Elizabeth Craig.

In the 1920s, the famous *Hutchinson's Dog Encyclopaedia* published this photo of the breed, identifying the breed as the "Dobermann Pinscher."

In Germany, Doberman Pinschers frequently were used in police and military work. In this photo, circa 1912, a German police dog trainer is putting a trainee through a practice session.

Portugal, Pitt-Milward went on to be the founding member of the International Dobermann Club.

Two of the first dogs imported from Germany by Fred and Julia Curnow were Derb and Beka von der Brunoburg. "Beka" was a black-and-tan bitch bred by Herr Carl Wienenkotter out of Frido v. Raufelsen and Unruh v. Sandberg. "Derb" was a black-and-tan male sired by Axel Germania, by Beka's dam Unruh v. Sandberg. The Curnows bred these two imports, which were the start of their foundation bloodlines.

Lionel Hamilton-Renwick's influence as an English breeder began when he imported Birling Bruno v. Ehrgarten from Switzerland. The dog was a black-and-tan male bred by Mr. W. Lenz. The breeding that later followed (Birling v. d. Heerhof and Birling Bruno v. Ehrgarten) would produce the first Dobermann male champion in the United Kingdom.

The Curnow kennel began to grow in quality and reputation shortly after acquiring Prinses Anja v't Scheepjeskerk. This bitch was bred by Mrs. Kniff Dermout. "Prinses" was a daughter from the famous Dutch and Int. Ch. Graaf Dagobert v. Neerlands Stam. She was later bred to Bruno of Tavey and produced Britain's first and only show and obedience champion, Dual Ch. Jupiter of Tavey.

Mary Porterfield and Sgt. Harry Darbyshire of Bowesmoor Kennels would later become a strong Dobermann force in England. Bowesmoor Kennels specialized in breeding and training working dogs, and acquired Ulf v. Margaretenhof and Donathe v. Begertal. These two dogs would have a tremendous influence on the "working" potential of the breed. Darbyshire trained and handled "Ulf" for the Surrey Police Dog Section. This dog would later become the first Dobermann working-trial champion.

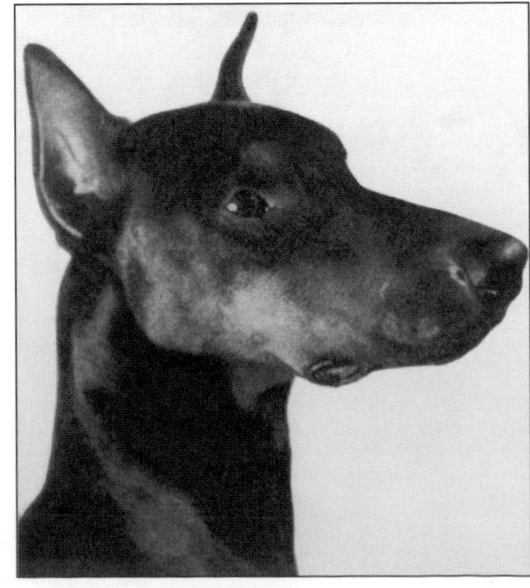

The Doberman Pinscher was very rare in the U.K. until after World War II. This is an early German import photographed in England in the mid-1920s.

By the 1950s, the breed began to increase in both popularity and quality in the show ring. In 1950, there were nine Dobermanns that participated at Crufts. By 1952, there were fifteen entries, but only two classes, Novice Dog or Bitch and Open Dog or Bitch. They were judged by H. G. Sanders, and the Best of Breed winner was Hamilton-Renwick's Birling Rachel. The start of the Challenge Certificate also began at Crufts in 1952. Leo Wilson (founding member of the Dobermann Club) gave the first certificate to a bitch named Elegant of Tavey, who later went on to be the breed's first U.K. champion.

At the turn of the century in eastern Switzerland, the foresters took Doberman Pinschers with them as guards and companions. Doberman Pinschers were also used for pulling wagons and sleds, along with carrying loads for the foresters.

The Dobermann, as the breed is called in the U.K., has natural drop ears; ear-cropping is banned in that country.

CHARACTERISTICS OF THE DOBERMAN PINSCHER

IS THE DOBERMAN PINSCHER THE RIGHT DOG FOR YOU?

If you're interested in acquiring a dog that is shy, disobedient and high-strung, the Doberman Pinscher is not for you. Instead, this magnificent breed is the complete opposite. The Doberman Pinscher is an alert, loyal, intelligent working dog that is as affectionate and responsive as any breed in existence. Its great muscular physique, striking color and willingness to please its owner have certainly contributed to its reputation. Although its popularity fluctuates from year to year, it continues to be one of the most desired breeds of dog in the world. It is the only breed of dog that was bred specifically to protect man, and it has successfully done just that for over a hundred years in many different countries.

The Doberman Pinscher is a fun-loving, playful dog who welcomes a daily game of fetch with his owner.

PERSONALITY AND TEMPERAMENT

This watchful, fearless, biddable athlete is one of the most (if not the most) versatile working breeds. It can be trained to compete in obedience trials and agility, and is a superlative show dog. The dog's desire to work for his owner, and the fact that he is easily trained, has enabled the breed to perform exceptionally well as a police and war dog. Police departments across the world continue to use the breed in their established K-9 units to track and apprehend criminals. The U.S. Marines and other branches of the military used the breed for various assignments during World War II. In fact, World War II was where the Doberman Pinscher gained its reputation as a fierce canine with a savage disposition. This unfortunate stigma is for the most part more myth than fact, especially in the United States and the United Kingdom.

When trained and conditioned correctly, the Doberman Pinscher is a well-balanced, trustworthy family dog. His loyalty to his

Doberman Pinschers must be socialized with children when the dogs are young. When reared within a household with children, Doberman Pinschers willingly and lovingly accept the children as their own.

loved ones and family members is unsurpassed. The breed brings constant devotion and affection to those who are willing to accept it. The fact that the breed is sometimes feared and distrusted is rather disappointing. To understand the Doberman Pinscher is to understand its temperament. As a watchdog and guard dog, its function and main priority is to protect. This protection includes your property and the individuals that are fortunate enough to share this space with the dog. Responsible training and early socialization are important in keeping the breed's protective nature in check. "To protect" does not mean that the dog should be trained to attack and bite intruders, or, even worse, assault friends or loving family members. If a Dobe is too aggressive and shows signs of unreliability, he can be extremely dangerous to everyone around him.

THE DOBERMAN PINSCHER AND CHILDREN

One of the very first questions that usually occurs before a family purchases a dog of any sort is the breed's adaptability to children. Even if there are not any children living in the home in which the dog is to be kept, it is likely that the dog will at some point be exposed to them. Once again, early socialization is extremely important to the breed's willing-

"V" STANDS FOR VERSATILE

The Doberman Pinscher excels in many different areas. The breed participates in conformation, obedience, agility, flyball, ring sport, Schutzhund, tracking, search and rescue, guiding the blind, therapy, hunting, herding and seizure alert. Few breeds can compare with its versatility.

ness to accept children and any other unfamiliar individuals that cross his path. If the dog is purchased at an early age (eight to ten weeks), the adaptability will be much easier. If the breed is acquired at a later age, and has already developed a mistrust or dislike for children, you could have a problem. The young Doberman Pinscher will quickly accept children as cherished family members and will socialize with them from the beginning, while practicing his genetic protective nature. For the older dog, it may take more time for a trusting relationship between child and dog to develop.

CONDITIONING AND EXERCISING YOUR DOBERMAN PINSCHER

Before you rush out and choose the Doberman Pinscher as your next pet, there are many things to consider. Are you the right person for this dog? Do you have an active lifestyle? Can you confidently control this strong, physically fit animal? Do you have the space to accommodate the Dobe's strenuous exercise requirements? These are the types of questions that you must carefully consider before making any drastic decisions, and before committing yourself to the obligations associated with dog ownership.

The ideal owner for a Doberman Pinscher is active and athletic, with plenty of time to spend exercising and conditioning her canine companion.

Although the Doberman Pinscher adjusts well to both city and country living, it is a large, active breed that needs adequate space to run to maintain its utmost physical condition. If a large yard is not available for the dog to burn off energy, a long, brisk walk in a park or open field must be part of your daily routine. Not only is physical exercise very important to the breed, but the same can be said for its mental exercise. The Doberman Pinscher is a highly intelligent breed that requires mental stimulation and constant challenges. If the Doberman Pinscher's mental capacity isn't stimulated, the dog will get bored rather quickly and look for ways to entertain himself, which usually results in destructive behavior at the owner's expense

TAILS AND EARS

The Doberman Pinscher's tail is customarily docked at the first or second joint, usually when the dog is about three to four days old. This practice has become frowned upon in certain European nations. Likewise, ear cropping, which is traditional in the U.S., has been banned in the U.K. and other European nations for many years.

RESPONSIBILITIES OF OWNERSHIP

For obvious safety reasons, the need to have full control of your Doberman Pinscher at all times cannot be overemphasized. There is nothing more dangerous than an individual who cannot physically control his own dog. In the case of this powerful breed, the danger is even more enhanced. The Doberman Pinscher is extremely intelligent and will test his owner's dominance from time to time as he

Doberman Pinschers can bond closely with children, developing strong protective, even parental, ties with the family youngsters.

matures. The breed's possessive, protective nature usually develops between six to nine months of age. As the dog matures, his temperament should become more trustworthy and reliable. For your own safety, and for the well-being of others, the dog must be kept secure both inside and outside the home. Loose dogs are considered grounds for apprehension and are an utmost danger to the public. The Doberman Pinscher should be kept on a leash at all times, and any free-running exercise should be done in areas where it can be properly controlled and away from the general public.

Two Doberman Pinschers accompanied this magnificent stallion into the main ring at a Paris dog show in order to announce Best in Show.

COLORS

There are four recognized Doberman Pinscher colors: black-and-tan, brown-and-tan, blue-and-tan and fawn-and-tan, which is often referred to as Isabella. The black-and-tan is the most common. The black-and-tan was the only acceptable color when the breed standard was first drawn up in Germany in 1899.

Owning a Doberman Pinscher can be a rewarding and satisfying experience. However, if you do decide to own one, you must accept the responsibilities that are associated with this ownership. Although it is a lovely breed with very few drawbacks, it is important to respect any concerns that your neighbors might have regarding its stability. Without showing any aggression whatsoever, even the quietest, best-mannered Doberman Pinscher can be very intimidating. Keep your dog quiet, well mannered and free from any undesirable behavior, and you should meet with very little resistance from your neighbors.

HEALTH CONCERNS OF THE DOBERMAN PINSCHER

In general, the Doberman Pinscher is a very healthy breed of dog. Nevertheless, there will be times when your dog may be affected by some type of illness. There are a number of minor ailments that you should be able to treat yourself, rather than having to make a trip to the veterinarian. If you are uncertain, it is always best to call the vet first, rather than attempt to treat something in which you have no expertise.

Like several other breeds of dog, the Doberman Pinscher can develop different types of skin and coat problems. Many skin disorders are a result of parasitic, fungal, hormonal or allergic reactions, and others are hereditary. "Blue Dobe" syndrome, or color dilution alopecia, is a persistent skin condition associated with blue Doberman Pinschers. Dogs are usually affected at birth, with bald patches occurring throughout various parts of the body. The condition is incurable, but some of the symptoms can be controlled and treated with medicated shampoos and ointments prescribed by your vet.

Von Willebrand's disease is a blood-clotting defect that affects many breeds, including the Doberman Pinscher. Depending on the severity of the disease, dogs may bruise easily or show signs of bleeding from the nose or mouth. The disease is hereditary and can be accurately tested for. Obviously, dogs that have a tendency to bleed should be tested before being considered for breeding purposes.

WATCH VS. GUARD

The Doberman Pinscher is used effectively as both a watchdog and a guard dog. Many people believe that a watchdog and a guard dog are the same thing and serve the same function. This is not true! The function of the watchdog is to alert his owner of possible danger or the presence of an intruder. A guard dog is specifically trained to protect the home or family—forcibly, if necessary.

Hypothyroidism is a very common disorder in all dogs. Some early indications of the disease include hair loss, lethargic behavior and dull or dry skin. A simple blood test will confirm the condition, and various medications will usually correct the problem.

Next to you, your vet will be your dog's best friend. Discuss the many aspects of the Doberman Pinscher's health with your vet and your breeder.

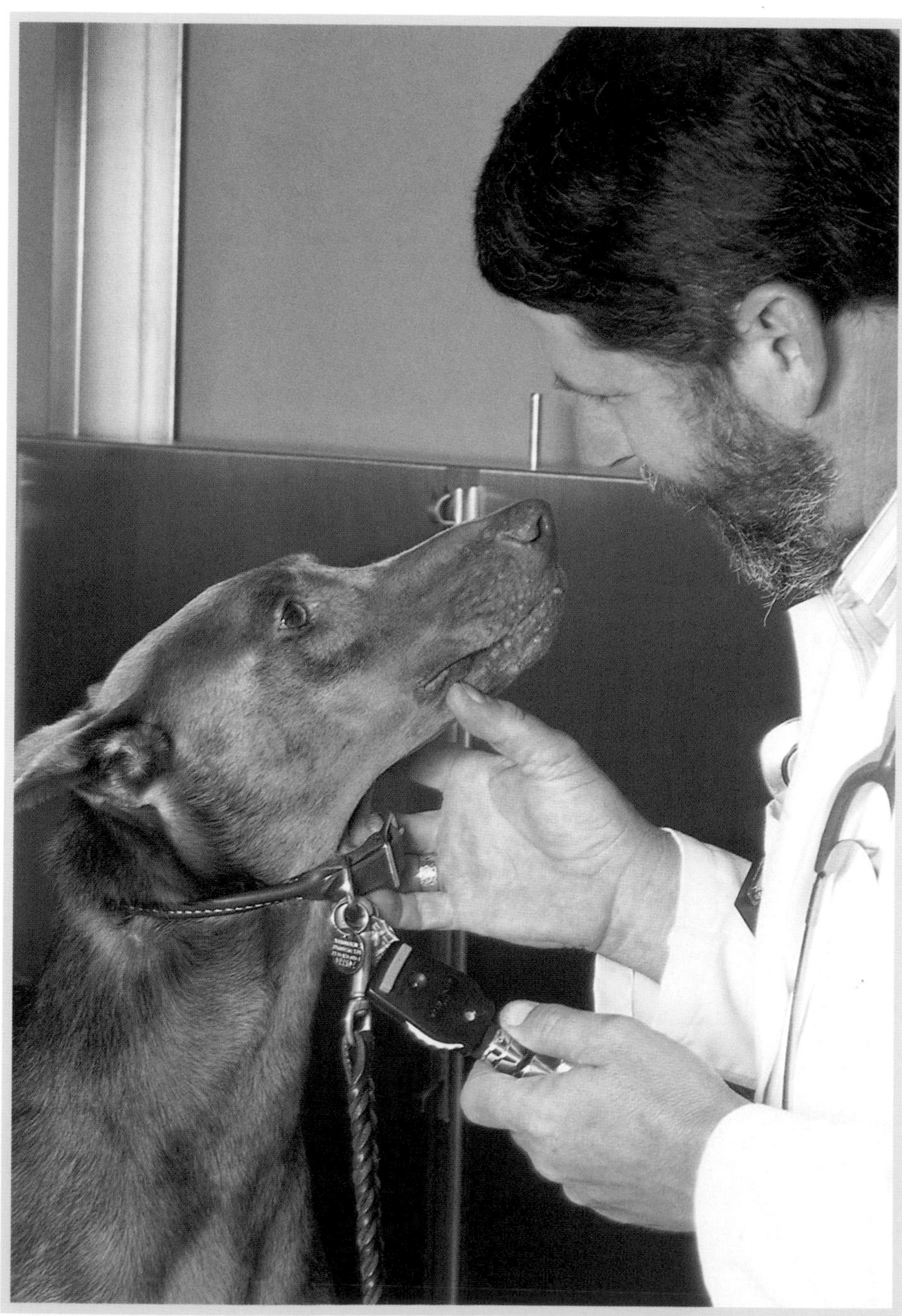

ACNE ALERT
The male Doberman Pinscher has a tendency to develop chin acne, which requires medicated shampoos and ointments to cure the condition.

Cervical vertical instability (CVI) or Wobbler syndrome is caused by an abnormality of the neck vertebrae. The condition puts pressure on the spinal cord, which causes instability in the dog's hind legs. Surprisingly, the condition has been found in many Doberman Pinschers in different degrees of severity. The cause of the problem remains unclear, and some experts speculate that the condition has to do with the dog's overall conformation, diet or perhaps even hereditary factors.

Progressive retinal atrophy (PRA) is caused by the degeneration of the cells of the retina of the eye. The condition is commonly found in sighthounds, but does occur less frequently in Doberman Pinschers. The first signs of the disease include the dog's loss of night vision. The condition will get worse until the dog is nearly or entirely blind. Unfortunately, there is no treatment for this condition and all dogs that test positive for the condition should be removed from breeding programs.

Dilated cardiomyopathy is a condition in which the heart muscle becomes thin and stretched and is unable to pump effectively. Affected dogs eventually succumb to heart failure. Some Doberman Pinschers with dilated cardiomyopathy have a defect in L-carnitine (an amino acid) levels in the heart muscle. These dogs occasionally respond to carnitine supplementation.

Wry mouth and zinc deficiency are not very common, but enough cases have been reported in Doberman Pinschers to warrant their inclusion in this section. Wry mouth is a dental abnormality in which an overshot or undershot condition affects only one side of the head. Zinc deficiency is the result of the dog's incapacity to utilize zinc. The most common symptoms are small bald spots on the dog's coat. A daily tablet of zinc sulphate will effectively correct the problem.

Discuss all these potential problems with your breeder and veterinarian. If your chosen breeder shows no concern about or knowledge of these problems, keep shopping!

Qualified, experienced breeders screen their breeding stock before producing a litter. Ask your breeder about health clearances on both the sire and dam before you buy your puppy.

BREED STANDARD FOR THE DOBERMAN PINSCHER

The Doberman Pinscher is a compactly built square dog, well muscled, powerful, yet elegant and proud of carriage.

A breed standard is a written description or idealistic blueprint of what the complete specimen of a particular breed should look like. Establishing a standard allows a breeder or judge to assess a dog against what is considered to be the perfect example for that breed. Without a standard, there would be no regard to quality or breed function, and the end result would be an ever-increasing divergence from the ideal Doberman Pinscher.

The breed standard is the best means to measure which Doberman Pinschers are considered to be top quality or "show quality," and which ones are considered average or "pet quality." A conformation judge at a dog show is expected to evaluate each of his or her entries against the breed standard. It is not as easy as it sounds, and in many cases it is rather difficult to measure different degrees of faults in two dogs, and decide which fault is worse than the other.

There are three main breed standards recognized and used by a majority of countries. They include the American breed standard (approved by the American Kennel Club in the U.S.), the British standard (established by The Kennel Club; used in the United Kingdom and other countries), and last, but not least, the Fédération Cynologique Intenationale (FCI) standard (used in

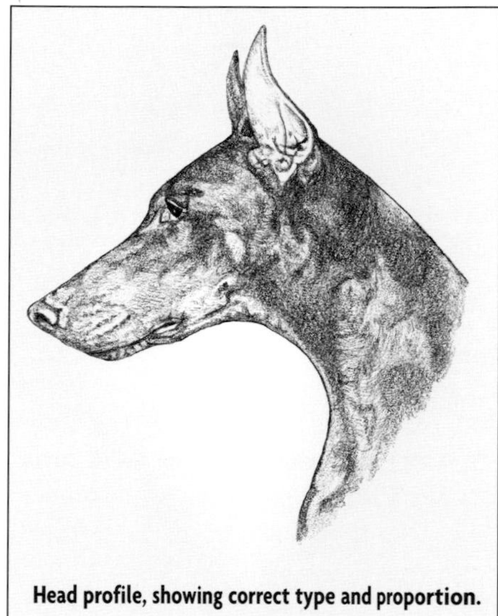
Head profile, showing correct type and proportion.

Europe and beyond). Other countries have their own breed standards, but in most cases they are a minor variation of one of the aforementioned. Here we include an excerpt from the AKC breed standard.

THE AMERICAN KENNEL CLUB STANDARD FOR THE DOBERMAN PINSCHER

General Appearance: The appearance is that of a dog of medium size, with a body that is square. Compactly built, muscular and powerful, for great endurance and speed. Elegant in appearance, of proud carriage, reflecting great nobility and temperament. Energetic, watchful, determined, alert, fearless, loyal and obedient.

Size, Proportion, Substance: Height at the withers: Dogs 26 to 28 inches, ideal about 27.5 inches; Bitches 24 to 26 inches, ideal about 25.5 inches. The height, measured vertically from the ground to the highest point of the withers, equalling the length measured horizontally from the forechest to the rear projection of the upper thigh. Length of head, neck and legs in proportion to length and depth of body.

Head: Long and dry, resembling a blunt wedge in both frontal and profile views. When seen from the front, the head widens gradually toward the base of the ears in a practically unbroken line. Eyes almond shaped, moderately deep set, with vigorous, energetic

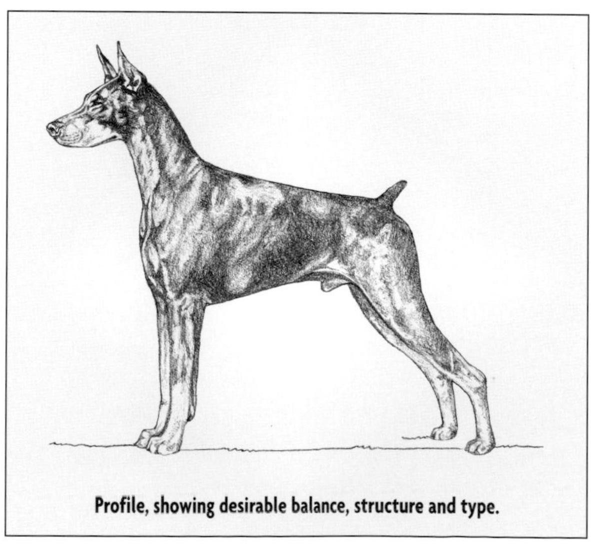
Profile, showing desirable balance, structure and type.

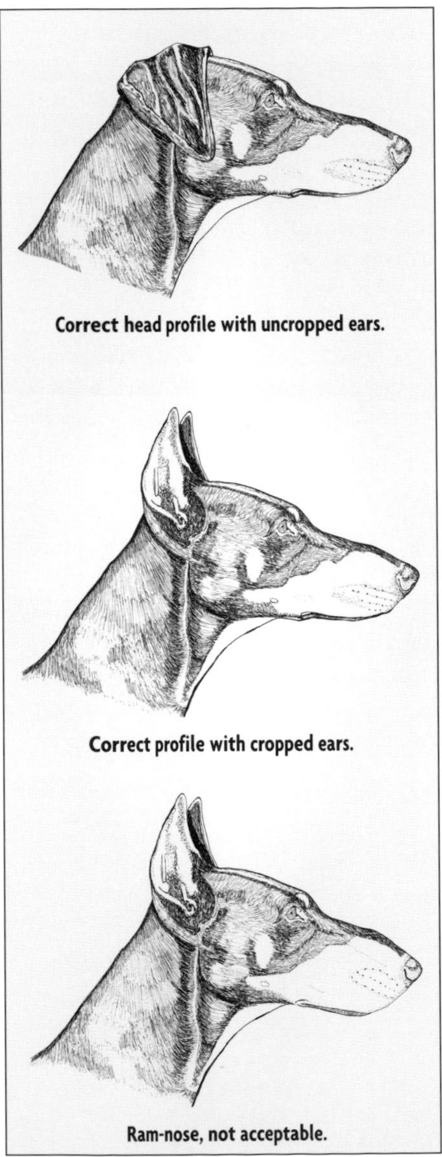
Correct head profile with uncropped ears.

Correct profile with cropped ears.

Ram-nose, not acceptable.

expression. Iris, of uniform color, ranging from medium to darkest brown in black dogs; in reds, blues, and fawns the color of the iris blends with that of the markings, the darkest shade being preferable in every case. Ears normally cropped and carried erect. The upper attachment of the ear, when held erect, is on a level with the top of the skull.

Top of skull flat, turning with slight stop to bridge of muzzle, with muzzle line extending parallel to top line of skull. Cheeks flat and muscular. Nose solid black on black dogs, dark brown on red ones, dark gray on blue ones, dark tan on fawns. Lips lying close to jaws. Jaws full and powerful, well filled under the eyes.

Teeth strongly developed and white. Lower incisors upright and touching inside of upper incisors a true scissors bite. 42 correctly placed teeth, 22 in the lower, 20 in the upper jaw. Distemper teeth shall not be penalized.

Neck, Topline, Body: Neck proudly carried, well muscled and dry. Well arched, with nape of neck widening gradually toward body. Length of neck proportioned to body and head. Withers pronounced and forming the highest point of the body. Back short, firm, of sufficient width, and muscular at the loins, extending in a straight line from withers to the slightly rounded croup.

Chest broad with forechest well defined. Ribs well sprung from the spine, but flattened in lower end to permit elbow clearance. Brisket reaching deep to the elbow. Belly well tucked up, extending in a curved line from the brisket. Loins wide and muscled. Hips broad and in proportion to body, breadth of hips being approximately equal to breadth of body at rib cage and shoulders.

Tail docked at approximately second joint, appears to be a continuation of the spine, and is carried only slightly above the horizontal when the dog is alert.

Forequarters: Shoulder blade sloping forward and downward at a 45-degree angle to the ground meets the upper arm at an angle of 90 degrees. Length of shoulder blade and upper arm are equal. Height from elbow to withers approximately equals height from ground to elbow. Legs seen from front and side, perfectly straight and parallel to each other from elbow to pastern; muscled and sinewy, with heavy bone. In normal pose and when gaiting, the elbows lie close to the brisket. Pasterns firm and almost perpendicular to the ground. Dewclaws may be removed. Feet well arched, compact, and catlike, turning neither in nor out.

Hindquarters: The angulation of the hindquarters balances that of the forequarters. Hip bone falls away from spinal column at an angle of about 30 degrees,

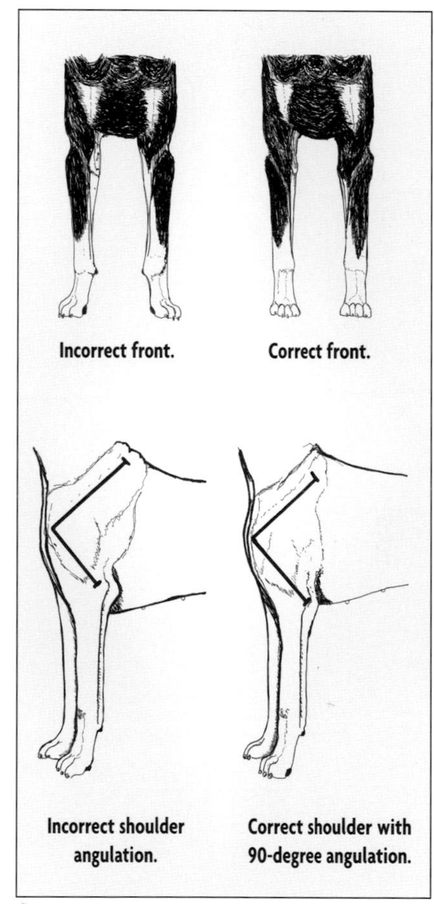

Incorrect front. Correct front.

Incorrect shoulder angulation. Correct shoulder with 90-degree angulation.

producing a slightly rounded, well filled-out croup. Upper shanks at right angles to the hip bones, are long, wide, and well muscled on both sides of thigh, with clearly defined stifles. Upper and lower shanks are of equal length. While the dog is at rest, hock to heel is perpendicular to the ground. Viewed from the rear, the legs are straight, parallel to each other, and wide

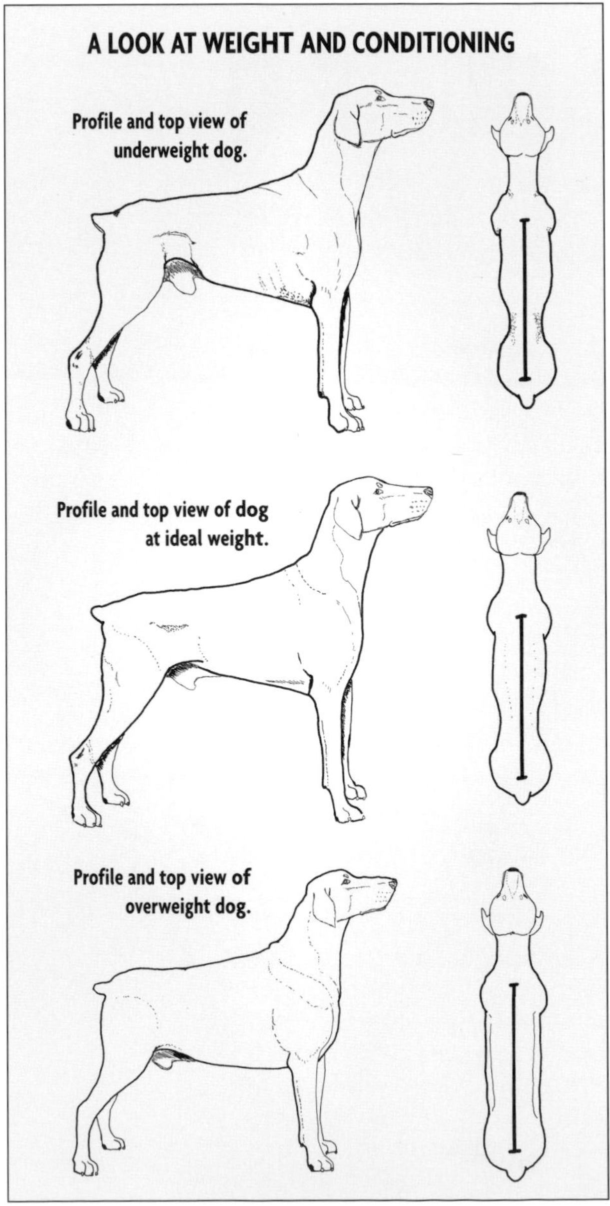

enough apart to fit in with a properly built body. Dewclaws, if any, are generally removed. Cat feet as on front legs, turning neither in nor out.

Coat: Smooth-haired, short, hard, thick and close lying. Invisible gray undercoat on neck permissible.

Color and Markings: Allowed Colors: Black, red, blue, and fawn (Isabella). Markings: Rust, sharply defined, appearing above each eye and on muzzle, throat and forechest, on all legs and feet, and below tail. White patch on chest, not exceeding one-half square inch, permissible.

Gait: Free, balanced, and vigorous, with good reach in the forequarters and good driving power in the hindquarters. When trotting, there is strong rear-action drive. Each rear leg moves in line with the foreleg on the same side. Rear and front legs are thrown neither in nor out. Back remains strong and firm. When moving at a fast trot, a properly built dog will single-track.

Temperament: Energetic, watchful, determined, alert, fearless, loyal and obedient. The judge shall dismiss from the ring any shy or vicious Doberman.

Disqualifications: Overshot more than three-sixteenth of an inch, undershot more than one-eighth of an inch. Four or more missing teeth. Dogs not of an allowed color.

YOUR PUPPY
DOBERMAN PINSCHER

WHERE TO BEGIN?

If you have decided that the Doberman Pinscher is the right dog for you, it's time to learn where to locate your dog of choice. The Doberman Pinscher is a popular breed, and acquiring a healthy, happy puppy should not be difficult if you look in the right places. The first step is to decide what type of dog you are interested in. Do you want a pet or a working dog? Do you want a dog that one day may be able to compete in the show ring? If you don't know of a reputable breeder in your area, it's best to contact the American Kennel Club, the Doberman Pinscher Club of America or a regional breed club. A comprehensive list is usually available in club publications, magazines and on the Internet. It's important to find a breeder who is established in the breed, practices outstanding dog ethics and has a strong commitment to the breed.

The search for a show-potential puppy is even more demanding than that for a pet puppy. Nonetheless, both show and pet puppies must be temperamentally and structurally fit. Never settle for a second-rate puppy.

ARE YOU PREPARED?

Unfortunately, when a puppy is bought by someone who does not take into consideration the time and attention that dog ownership requires, it is the puppy who suffers when he is either abandoned or placed in a shelter by a frustrated owner. So all of the "homework" you do in preparation for your pup's arrival will benefit you both. The more informed you are, the more you will know what to expect and the better equipped you will be to handle the ups and downs of raising a puppy. Hopefully, everyone in the household is willing to do his part in raising and caring for the pup. The anticipation of owning a dog often brings a lot of promises from excited family members: "I will walk him every day," "I will feed him," "I will house-train him," etc., but these things take time and effort, and promises can easily be forgotten once the novelty of the new pet has worn off.

MEETING THE BREEDER

Once you have located and contacted a breeder, make an appointment to visit his facilities. Any new prospective owners should bring along a list of questions about the breed and any other concerns they may have. If the breeder is reputable, he will take the time necessary to explain both the good and bad aspects of the breed, and help decide what type of dog may be suitable for you. A reputable breeder will accept a puppy back, without questions, should you decide that the dog is not the right one for you. Remember to be courteous and polite when asking questions, and keep in mind that the breeder has his own dogs' best interest in mind.

When choosing a breeder, reputation is much more important than convenience or location. An ideal place to find a reputable breeder is at a local dog show. Find out beforehand when the Doberman Pinschers are scheduled to be exhibited, and closely watch them being judged. After the judging is completed, kindly introduce yourself to some of the handlers or spectators present, and inquire about purchasing a dog. Most of the handlers and breeders in attendance will eagerly guide you in the right direction.

The Doberman Pinscher is a large working breed, capable of great strength and endurance.

Therefore, finding a dog with a sound temperament is extremely important. A dog that has not been properly socialized and trained as a puppy or adolescent can be extremely dangerous when placed in the wrong hands. A reputable Doberman Pinscher breeder should understand the importance of proper socialization and promote a sound socialization regimen in his puppy-rearing program.

Choosing a reputable breeder whom you can trust and turn to for assistance is essential. Fortunately, the majority of Doberman Pinscher breeders is devoted to their breed and concerned about its well-being. If you have difficulty finding a Doberman Pinscher breeder in your area who suits your needs, expand your search and make more contacts until you find someone with whom you are comfortable.

SELECTING A PUPPY

Now that you have contacted and met a breeder or two and made your choice about which breeder is best suited to your needs, it's time to visit the litter. It's not uncommon for new owners to be placed on a waiting list for a puppy for long periods of time, especially if the breeder has a reputation for producing good-quality dogs. Don't despair. The long wait should be worth it! It's better to be patient and acquire a dog that's suitable to your needs rather than to rush into a choice that you will certainly be unhappy with later.

Generally, you should look for a Doberman Pinscher puppy that

PUPPY APPEARANCE

Your puppy should have a well-fed appearance but not a distended abdomen, which may indicate worms or incorrect feeding, or both. The body should be firm, with a solid feel. The skin of the abdomen should be pale pink and clean, without signs of scratching or rash. Check the legs to see if the dewclaws have been removed, as this is usually done at a few days old.

Doberman litters are feisty and energetic, making your selection quite an entertaining process.

is happy, outgoing and active. The pup should be friendly, with an attractive coat, clear, dark eyes and an overall healthy appearance. Examine the teeth closely. If the puppy's teeth are not yet fully developed, check the gums to make sure the dog is not undershot or overshot. Doberman Pinschers have large litters, generally averaging between 8 and 12 puppies. Even after the breeder has chosen his own picks from the litter, you should be left with a handsome selection from which to choose. Beware of the shy or overly aggressive puppy. A Doberman Pinscher puppy should be assertive and confident, but not overly aggressive. Keep your emotions in check while purchasing your puppy. Don't let sentiment or emotion trap you into buying a dog that is shy or timid. Whenever possible, take a close look at the litter's parents. Do the parents look healthy? Do they appear like the handsome dogs in this book?

If you intend to show your dog, or plan on having him participate in obedience competition or another performance activity, there are many more considerations to take into account. Are you acquiring your Doberman Pinscher for the purpose of using him as a watchdog or guard dog? Do you plan on using him for police or military work? The parents of a future working dog should have excellent qualifications, including actual work experience as well as working titles in their pedigrees (such as SchH., UD, TD). Without these titles, there is no true indication that your new puppy will be capable of handling the specialized roles you may have planned for him.

Choosing a male or female Doberman Pinscher puppy is largely a matter of personal taste. Both sexes will respond to training at the same pace and will deliver the same outcome. The difference in size is noticeable, with males being considerably larger. The black and tan color pattern is one of the most striking color patterns of the breed. Depending on your taste, the brown and tan, blue and tan, and fawn and tan are also considered equally attractive.

The Doberman Pinscher is one of the most popular breeds in the world. Unfortunately, commercial breeders are attracted to the breed and there are many breeders more interested in producing a profit than in selling quality dogs. Be careful!

Breeders commonly allow visitors to see their litter by around the fourth or fifth week, and puppies leave for their new homes between the eighth and tenth week. Breeders who permit their puppies to leave early should be avoided. In many countries, it is against the law to sell a dog under the age of seven weeks. If a breeder is willing to sell a dog at such a young age, odds are there is a reason for this, and that reason is not likely favorable to the purchaser. Chances are the breeder is more interested in your money than his puppies' well-being.

Reputable breeders will spend significant amounts of time training and socializing their Doberman Pinscher youngsters. Exposing the puppies to many different elements will help them adjust to the world around them. It is not uncommon for a litter of puppies to be taken on short car rides, driven over to the homes of relatives or friends and exposed to other dogs and humans on a daily basis. Socializing is extremely important and encouraged. This is the only effective way that puppies will learn to successfully interact. Given the long history that dogs and humans have, bonding between the two species is natural but must be nurtured.

TEMPERAMENT COUNTS

Your selection of a good puppy can be determined by your needs. A show potential or a good pet? It is your choice. Every puppy, however, should be of good temperament. Although show-quality puppies are bred and raised with emphasis on physical conformation, responsible breeders strive for equally good temperament. Do not buy from a breeder who concentrates solely on physical beauty at the expense of personality.

A well-socialized Doberman Pinscher pup will grow attached to his owner immediately. It is not uncommon for the toddler to follow his owner from room to room. The Doberman Pinscher puppy wants nothing more than to be near you and please you. He is extremely loyal, and he will go to great lengths to please his owner.

TIME TO GO HOME

Breeders rarely release puppies until they are eight to ten weeks of age. This is an acceptable age for most breeds of dog, excepting toy breeds, which are not released until around 12 weeks, given their petite sizes. If a breeder has a puppy that is 12 weeks of age or older, he is likely well socialized and house-trained. Be sure that the pup is otherwise healthy before deciding to take him home.

COMMITMENT OF OWNERSHIP

After considering all of these factors, you have most likely already made some very important decisions about selecting your puppy. You have chosen the Doberman Pinscher, which means that you have decided which characteristics you want in a dog and what type of dog will best fit into your family and lifestyle. If you have selected a breeder, you have gone a step further—you have done your research and found a responsible, conscientious person who breeds quality Doberman Pinschers and who should be a reliable source of help as you and your puppy adjust to life together. If you have observed a litter in action, you have obtained a firsthand look at the dynamics of a puppy "pack" and, thus, you should have learned about each pup's individual personality—perhaps you have even found one that particularly appeals to you.

However, even if you have not yet found the Doberman Pinscher puppy of your dreams, observing pups will help you learn to recognize certain behavior and to determine what a pup's behavior indicates about his temperament. You will be able to pick out which pups are the leaders, which ones are less outgoing, which ones are confident, which ones are shy, playful, friendly, aggressive, etc. Equally as important, you will learn to recognize what a healthy pup should look and act like. All of these things will help you in your search, and when you find the Doberman Pinscher that was meant for you, you will know it!

Researching your breed, selecting a responsible breeder and observing as many pups as possible are all important steps on the way to dog ownership. It may seem like a lot of effort...and you have not even brought the pup home yet! Remember, though, you cannot be too careful when it comes to deciding on the type of dog you want and finding out about your prospective pup's background. Buying a puppy is not—or should not be—just another whimsical purchase. This is one instance in which you actually do get to choose your own family! You may be thinking that buying a puppy should be fun—it should not be so serious and so much work. Keep in mind that your puppy is not a cuddly stuffed toy or decorative lawn ornament, but a creature that will become a real

PEDIGREE VS. REGISTRATION CERTIFICATE

Too often new owners are confused between these two important documents. Your puppy's pedigree, essentially a family tree, is a written record of a dog's genealogy of three generations or more. The pedigree will show you the names as well as performance titles of all the dogs in your pup's background. Your breeder must provide you with a registration application, with his part properly filled out. You must complete the application and send it to the AKC with the proper fee. The seller must provide you with complete records to identify the puppy. The AKC requires that the seller provide the buyer with the following: breed; sex, color and markings; date of birth; litter number (when available); names and registration numbers of the parents; breeder's name; and date sold or delivered.

Are you ready for a ten-or-more-year commitment to walk into your life? Any dog is a huge responsibility—a Doberman Pinscher is even larger than that!

ARE YOU A FIT OWNER?
If the breeder from whom you are buying a puppy asks you a lot of personal questions, do not be insulted. Such a breeder wants to be sure that you will be a fit provider for his puppy.

member of your family. You will come to realize that, while buying a puppy is a pleasurable and exciting endeavor, it is not something to be taken lightly. Relax...the fun will start when the pup comes home!

Always keep in mind that a puppy is nothing more than a baby in a furry disguise...a baby who is virtually helpless in a human world and who trusts his owner for fulfillment of his basic needs for survival. In addition to food, water and shelter, your pup needs care, protection, guidance and love. If you are not prepared to commit to this, then you are not prepared to own a dog.

"Wait a minute," you say. "How hard could this be? All of my neighbors own dogs and they seem to be doing just fine. Why should I have to worry about all of this?" Well, you should not worry about it; in fact, you will probably find that once your Doberman Pinscher pup gets used to his new home, he will fall into his place in the family quite naturally. But it never hurts to emphasize the commitment of dog ownership. With some time and patience, it is really not too difficult to raise a curious and exuberant Doberman Pinscher pup to be a well-adjusted and well-mannered adult dog—a dog that could be your most loyal friend.

PREPARING PUPPY'S PLACE IN YOUR HOME

Researching your breed and finding a breeder are only two aspects of the "homework" you will have to do before bringing your Doberman Pinscher puppy home. You will also have to prepare your home and family for the new addition. Much like you would prepare a nursery for a newborn baby, you will need to designate a place in your home that will be the puppy's own. How you prepare your home will depend on how much freedom the dog will be allowed. Will he be confined to one room or a specific area in the house, or will he be allowed to roam as he pleases? Will he spend most of his time in the house or will he be primarily an outdoor dog? Whatever you decide, you must ensure that he has a place that he can "call his own."

When you bring your new puppy into your home, you are bringing him into what will become his home as well. Obviously, you did not buy a puppy so that he could take control of the house, but in order for a puppy to grow into a stable, well-adjusted dog, he has to feel comfortable in his surroundings. Remember, he is leaving the warmth and security of his mother and littermates, as well as the familiarity of the only place he has ever known, so it is important to make his transition as easy as possible. By preparing a place in your home for the puppy, you are making him feel as welcome as possible in a strange new place. It should not take him long to get used to it, but the sudden shock of being transplanted is somewhat traumatic for a young pup. Imagine how a small child would feel in the same situation—that is how your puppy must be feeling. It is up to you to

YOUR SCHEDULE . . .

If you lead an erratic, unpredictable life, with daily or weekly changes in your work requirements, consider the problems of owning a puppy. The new puppy has to be fed regularly, socialized (loved, petted, handled, introduced to other people) and, most importantly, allowed to go outdoors for house-training. As the dog gets older, he can become more tolerant of deviations in his feeding and relief schedule.

Puppies from an experienced breeder will have the advantages of socialization and crate training. This litter of Doberman Pinschers is spending some quality time with a young visitor.

reassure him and to let him know, "Little buddy, you are going to like it here!"

WHAT YOU SHOULD BUY

CRATE

To someone unfamiliar with the use of crates in dog training, it may seem like punishment to put a dog in a crate, but this is not the case at all. Crates are not cruel—crates have many humane and highly effective uses in dog care and training. For example, crate training is a very popular and very successful housebreaking method. A crate can keep your dog safe during travel and, perhaps most importantly, a crate provides your dog with a place of his own in your home. It serves as a "doggie bedroom" of sorts—your Doberman Pinscher can curl up in his crate when he wants to sleep or when he just needs a break. Many dogs sleep in their crates overnight. With soft bedding and his favorite toy, a crate becomes a cozy pseudo-den for your dog. Like his ancestors, he too will seek out the comfort and retreat of a den—you just happen to be providing him with something a bit more luxurious than what his early ancestors enjoyed.

As far as purchasing a crate, the type that you buy is up to you. It will most likely be one of the two most popular types: wire or fiberglass. There are advantages and disadvantages to each type. For example, a wire crate is more open, allowing the air to flow through and affording the dog a

CRATE-TRAINING TIPS

During crate training, you should partition off the section of the crate in which the pup stays. If he is given too big an area, this will hinder your training efforts. Crate training is based on the fact that a dog does not like to soil his sleeping quarters, so it is ineffective to keep a pup in a crate that is so big that he can eliminate in one end and get far enough away from it to sleep. Also, you want to make the crate den-like for the pup. Blankets and a favorite toy will make the crate cozy for the small pup; as he grows, you may want to evict some of his "roommates" to make more room. It will take some coaxing at first, but be patient. Given some time to get used to it, your pup will adapt to his new home-within-a-home quite nicely.

PHOTO COURTESY OF DOSKOCIL.

Your local pet shop should have a wide variety of crates in various sizes. Purchase the largest crate available to house your Doberman Pinscher.

view of what is going on around him. A fiberglass crate, however, is sturdier and can double as a travel crate since it provides more protection for the dog. The size of the crate is another thing to consider. Puppies do not stay puppies forever—in fact, sometimes it seems as if they grow right before your eyes. A small crate may be fine for a very young Doberman Pinscher pup, but it will not do him much good for long! Unless you have the money and the inclination to buy a new crate every time your pup has a growth spurt, it is better to get one that will accommodate your dog both as a pup and at full size. A medium to large-size crate will be necessary for a full-grown Doberman Pinscher, who stands approximately 28 inches high.

BEDDING

A crate pad in the dog's crate will help the dog feel more at home and you may also like to add a small blanket. This will take the place of the leaves, twigs, etc., that the pup would use in the wild to make a den; the pup can make his own "burrow" in the crate. Although your pup is far removed from his den-making ancestors, the denning instinct is still a part of his genetic makeup. Second, until you bring your pup home, he has been sleeping amid the warmth of his mother and littermates, and while a blanket is not the same as a warm, breathing body, it still provides heat and something with which to snuggle. You will want to wash your pup's bedding frequently in case he has an accident in his crate, and replace or remove any blanket that becomes ragged and starts to fall apart.

Toys

Toys are a must for dogs of all ages, especially for curious playful pups. Puppies are the "children" of the dog world, and what child does not love toys? Chew toys provide enjoyment to both dog and owner—your dog will enjoy playing with his favorite toys, while you will enjoy the fact that they distract him from your expensive shoes and leather sofa. Puppies love to chew; in fact, chewing is a physical need for pups as they are teething, and everything looks appetizing! The full range of your possessions—from old dish rag to Oriental carpet—are fair game in the eyes of a teething pup. Puppies are not all that discerning when it comes to finding something to literally "sink their teeth into"—everything tastes great!

Provide your puppy with safe chew toys so that he will not eat your slippers or worse!

Doberman Pinscher puppies are fairly aggressive chewers and only the hardest, strongest toys should be offered to them. Breeders advise owners to resist stuffed toys, because they can become destuffed in no time. The overly excited pup may ingest the stuffing, which is neither nutritious nor digestible.

Similarly, squeaky toys are quite popular, but must be avoided

QUALITY FOOD

The cost of food must be mentioned. All dogs need a good-quality food with an adequate supply of protein to develop their bones and muscles properly. Most dogs are not picky eaters but, unless fed properly, can quickly succumb to skin problems.

In addition to a crate, your Doberman Pinscher will welcome a soft bed to relax in while spending time with his family.

for the Doberman Pinscher. Perhaps a squeaky toy can be used as an aid in training, but not for free play. If a pup "disembowels" one of these, the small plastic squeaker inside can be dangerous if swallowed. Monitor the condition of all your pup's toys carefully and get rid of any that have been chewed to the point of becoming potentially dangerous.

Be careful of natural bones, which have a tendency to splinter into sharp, dangerous pieces. Also be careful of rawhide, which can turn into pieces that are easy to swallow or into a mushy mess on your carpet.

Leash

A nylon leash is probably the best option as it is the most resistant to puppy teeth should your pup take a liking to chewing on his leash. Of course, this is a habit that should be nipped in the bud, but if your pup likes to chew on his leash he has a very slim chance of being able to chew through the strong nylon. Nylon leashes are also lightweight, which is good for a young Doberman Pinscher who is just getting used to the idea of walking on a leash. For everyday walking and safety purposes, the nylon leash is a good choice. Of course, there are special leashes for training purposes, and specially made harnesses for the working Doberman Pinscher, but these are not necessary for routine walks.

Collar

Your pup should get used to wearing a collar all the time since you will want to attach his ID tags to it. You have to attach the leash to something! A lightweight nylon collar is a good choice; make sure that it fits snugly enough so that the pup cannot wriggle out of it, but is loose enough so that it will not be uncomfortably tight around the pup's neck. You should be able to fit a finger between the pup and the collar. It may take some time for your pup to get used to wearing the collar, but soon he will not even notice that it is there. Choke collars are made for training, but should only be used by an experienced handler.

Food and Water Bowls

Your pup will need two bowls, one for food and one for water. You may want two sets of bowls, one for inside and one for outside, depending on where the dog will be fed and where he will be spending most of his time. Stainless steel or sturdy plastic bowls are popular choices. Plastic bowls are more chewable. Dogs tend not to chew on the steel variety, which can be sterilized. It is important to buy sturdy bowls since anything is in danger of being chewed by puppy teeth and you do not want your dog to be constantly chewing apart his bowl (for his safety and for your purse!).

Cleaning Supplies

Expect to have to clean up potty mishaps for the first few weeks with your new pup. This is okay in the beginning because the

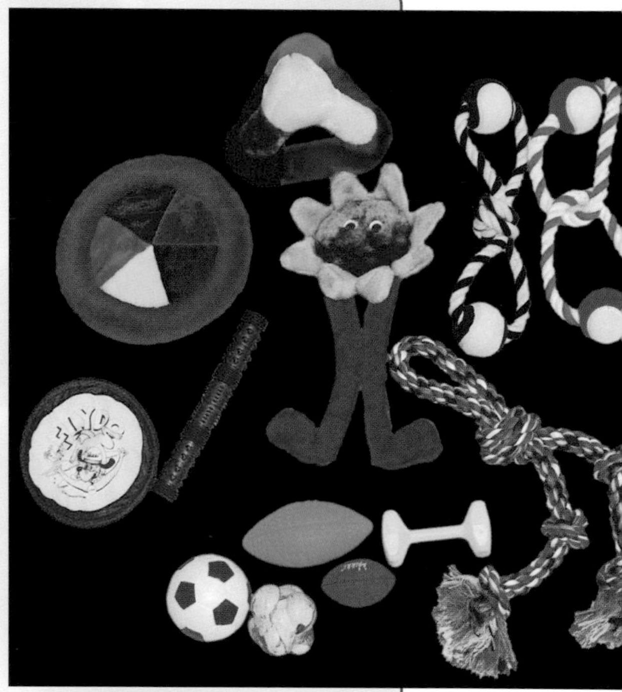

Purchase chew toys for your Doberman Pinscher that are strong and durable, able to withstand the powerful jaws of the growing Doberman Pinscher.

TOYS, TOYS, TOYS!

With a big variety of dog toys available, and so many that look like they would be a lot of fun for a dog, be careful in your selection. It is amazing what a set of puppy teeth can do to an innocent-looking toy; so, obviously, safety is a major consideration. Be sure to choose the most durable products that you can find. Hard nylon bones and toys are a safe bet, and many of them are offered in different scents and flavors that will be sure to capture your dog's attention. It is always fun to play a game of fetch with your dog, and there are balls and flying discs that are specially made to withstand dog teeth.

Your local pet shop will probably have a wide variety of leashes from which you can choose. For the Doberman Pinscher purchase the strongest and sturdiest leash available. Quality pet products are necessities when you own a Doberman Pinscher.

puppy does not know any better. All you can do is be prepared to clean up any "accidents." Old rags, paper towels, newspapers and a safe disinfectant are good to have on hand.

Beyond the Basics

The items previously discussed are the bare necessities. You will find out what else you need as you go along—grooming supplies, flea/tick protection, baby gates to partition a room, etc. These things will vary depending on your situation, but it is important that you have everything you need to feed and make your Doberman Pinscher comfortable in his first few days at home.

PUPPY-PROOFING YOUR HOME

Aside from making sure that your Doberman Pinscher will be comfortable in your home, you also have to make sure that your home is safe for your Doberman Pinscher. This means taking precautions that your pup will not get into anything he should not get into and that there is nothing within his reach that may harm him should he sniff it, chew it, inspect it, etc. This probably seems obvious since, while you are primarily concerned with your pup's safety, at the same time you do not want your belongings to be ruined. Breakables should be placed out of reach if your dog is to have full run of the house. If he

FINANCIAL RESPONSIBILITY

Grooming tools, collars, leashes, a crate, a dog bed and, of course, toys will be expenses to you when you first obtain your pup, and the cost will continue throughout your dog's lifetime. If your puppy damages or destroys your possessions (as most puppies surely will!) or something belonging to a neighbor, you can calculate additional expense. There is also flea and pest control, which every dog owner faces more than once. You must be able to handle the financial responsibility of owning a dog.

The BUCKLE COLLAR is the standard collar used for everyday purposes. Be sure that you adjust the buckle on growing puppies. Check it every day. It can become too tight overnight! These collars can be made of leather or nylon. Attach your dog's identification tags to this collar.

The CHOKE COLLAR is designed for training. It is constructed of highly polished steel so that it slides easily through the stainless steel loop. The idea is that the dog controls the pressure around his neck and he will stop pulling if the collar becomes uncomfortable. *Never* leave a choke collar on your dog when not training.

The HALTER is for a trained dog that has to be restrained to prevent running away, chasing a cat and the like. Considered the most humane of all collars, it is frequently used on smaller dogs for which collars are not comfortable.

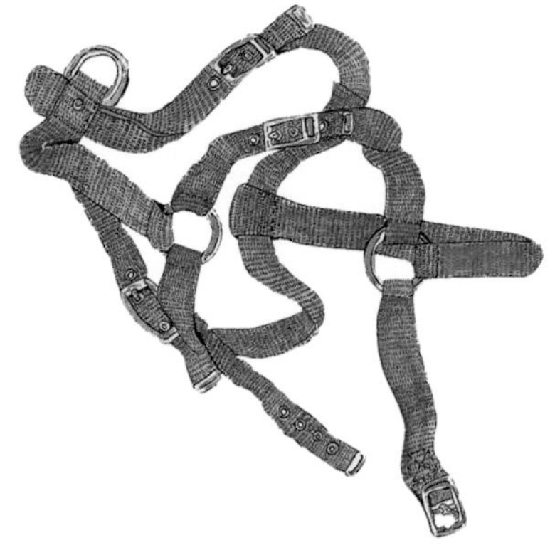

Pet shops offer a variety of bowls from which to choose. Purchase large, sturdy food and water bowls that can be cleaned easily.

PHOTO COURTESY OF MIKKI PET PRODUCTS.

is to be limited to certain places within the house, keep any potentially dangerous items in the "off-limits" areas. An electrical cord can pose a danger should the puppy decide to taste it—and who is going to convince a pup that it would not make a great chew toy? Cords should be fastened tightly against the wall. If your dog is going to spend time in a crate, make sure that there is nothing near his crate that he can reach if he sticks his curious little nose or paws through the openings. Just as you would with a child, keep all household cleaners and chemicals where the pup cannot reach them.

It is also important to make sure that the outside of your home is safe. Of course your puppy should never be unsupervised, but a pup let loose in the yard will want to run and explore, and he should be granted that freedom. Do not let a fence give you a false sense of security; you would be surprised

PUPPY-PROOFING

Thoroughly puppy-proof your house before bringing your puppy home. Never use roach or rodent poisons in any area accessible to the puppy. Avoid the use of toilet cleaners. Most dogs are born with "toilet sonar" and will take a drink if the lid is left open. Also keep the trash secured and out of reach.

how crafty (and persistent) a dog can be in working out how to dig under and squeeze his way through small holes, or to jump or climb over a fence. The remedy is to make the fence high enough so that it really is impossible for your dog to get over it (about 6 feet should suffice), and well-embedded into the ground. Be sure to repair or secure any gaps in the fence. Check the fence periodically to ensure that it is in good shape and make repairs as needed; a very determined pup may return to the same spot to "work on it" until he is able to get through.

CHEMICAL TOXINS

Scour your garage for potential puppy dangers. Remove weed killers, pesticides and antifreeze materials. Antifreeze is highly toxic and a few drops can kill a puppy or an adult dog. The sweet taste attracts the animal, who will quickly consume it from the floor or pavement.

FIRST TRIP TO THE VET

You have picked out your puppy, and your home and family are ready. Now all you have to do is collect your Doberman Pinscher from the breeder and the fun begins, right? Well...not so fast. Something else you need to prepare is your pup's first trip to the veterinarian. Perhaps the breeder can recommend someone in the area who specializes in large-breed dogs, or maybe you know some other Doberman Pinscher owners who can suggest a good vet. Either way, you should have an appointment arranged for your pup before you pick him up and plan on taking him for an examination before taking him home.

The pup's first visit will consist of an overall examination to make sure that the pup does not have any problems that are not apparent to you. The veterinarian will also set up a schedule for the pup's vaccinations; the breeder will inform you of which

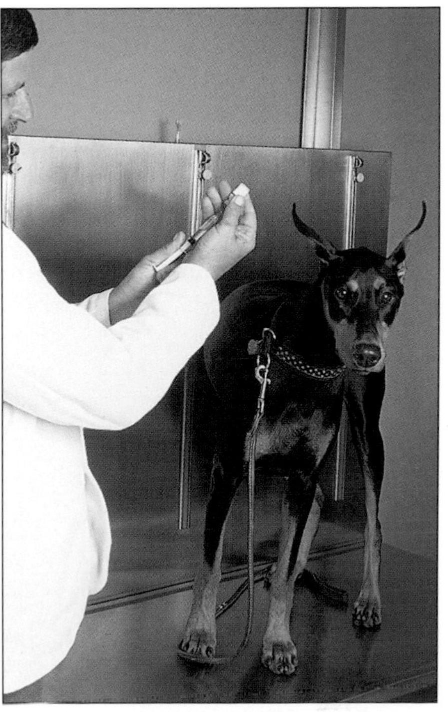

Your vet will schedule and keep a record of your puppy's vaccinations. It's a good idea to keep your own records of all inoculations given to your Doberman Pinscher.

NATURAL TOXINS

Examine your lawn and home landscaping before bringing your puppy home. Many varieties of plants have leaves, stems or flowers that are toxic if ingested, and you can depend on a curious puppy to investigate them. Ask your vet for information on poisonous plants or research them at your library.

ones the pup has already received and the vet can continue from there.

INTRODUCTION TO THE FAMILY

Everyone in the house will be excited about the puppy's coming home and will want to pet him and play with him, but it is best to make the introduction low-key so as not to overwhelm the puppy. He is apprehensive already. It is the first time he has been separated from his dam and the breeder, and the ride to your home is likely the first time he has been in a car. The last thing you want to do is smother him, as this will only frighten him further. This is not to say that human contact is not extremely necessary at this stage, because this is the time when a connection between the pup and his human family is formed. Gentle petting and soothing words should help console him, as well as just putting him down and letting him explore on his own (under your watchful eye, of course).

The pup may approach the family members or may busy himself with exploring for a while. Gradually, each person should spend some time with the pup, one at a time, crouching down to get as close to the pup's level as possible and letting him sniff their hands and petting him gently. He definitely needs human attention and he needs to be touched—this is how to form an immediate bond. Just remember that the pup is experiencing a lot of things for the first time, at the same time. There are new people, new noises, new smells and new things to investigate: so be gentle, be affectionate and be as comforting as you can be.

YOUR PUP'S FIRST NIGHT HOME

You have traveled home with your new charge safely in his

crate. He's been to the vet for a thorough check-up, he's been weighed, his papers examined; perhaps he's even been vaccinated and wormed as well. He's met the family, licked the whole family, including the excited children and the less-than-happy cat. He's explored his area, his new bed, the yard and anywhere else he's been permitted. He's eaten his first meal at home and relieved himself in the proper place. He's heard lots of new sounds, smelled new friends and seen more of the outside world than ever before.

That was just the first day! He's tuckered out and is ready for bed...or so you think!

It's puppy's first night and you are ready to say "Good night"—keep in mind that this is puppy's first night ever to be sleeping alone. His dam and littermates are no longer at paw's length and he's a bit scared, cold and lonely. Be reassuring to your new family member. This is not the time to spoil him and give in to his inevitable whining.

Puppies whine. They whine to let others know where they are and hopefully to get company out of it. Place your pup in his new bed or crate in his room and close the door. Mercifully, he may fall asleep without a peep. When the

TOXIC PLANTS

Many plants can be toxic to dogs. If you see your dog carrying a piece of vegetation in his mouth, approach him in a quiet, disinterested manner, avoid eye contact, pet him and gradually remove the plant from his mouth. Alternatively, offer him a treat and maybe he'll drop the plant on his own accord. Be sure no toxic plants are growing in your own garden.

Your Doberman Pinscher puppy totally relies on you for his safety and shelter. Learn to be a responsible dog owner.

What's itching your puppy? Sometimes a pup just needs a good scratch, but sometimes allergens, parasites or other irritants can cause problems that warrant a trip to the vet.

inevitable occurs, ignore the whining: he is fine. Be strong and keep his interest in mind. Do not allow yourself to feel guilty and visit the pup. He will fall asleep eventually.

Many breeders recommend placing a piece of bedding from his former home in his new bed so that he recognizes the scent of his littermates. Others still advise placing a hot water bottle in his bed for warmth. This latter may be a good idea provided the pup doesn't attempt to suckle—he'll get good and wet and may not fall asleep so fast.

Puppy's first night can be somewhat stressful for the pup and his new family. Remember that you are setting the tone of nighttime at your house. Unless you want to play with your pup every night at 10 p.m., midnight and 2 a.m., don't initiate the habit. Your family will thank you, and so will your pup!

PREVENTING PUPPY PROBLEMS

SOCIALIZATION

Now that you have done all of the preparatory work and have helped your pup get accustomed to his new home and family, it is about

STRESS-FREE

Some experts in canine health advise that stress during a dog's early years of development can compromise and weaken his immune system, and may trigger the potential for a shortened life. They emphasize the need for happy and stress-free growing-up years.

THE RIDE HOME

Taking your dog from the breeder to your home in a car can be a very uncomfortable experience for both of you. The puppy will have been taken from his warm, friendly, safe environment and brought into a strange new environment—an environment that moves! Be prepared for loose bowels, urination, crying, whining and even fear biting. With proper love and encouragement when you arrive home, the stress of the trip should quickly disappear.

time for you to have some fun! Socializing your Doberman Pinscher pup gives you the opportunity to show off your new friend, and your pup gets to reap the benefits of being an adorable creature that people will want to pet and, in general, think is absolutely precious!

Besides getting to know his new family, your puppy should be exposed to other people, animals and situations, but of course he must not come into close contact with dogs you don't know well until his course of injections is fully complete. This will help him become well adjusted as he grows up and less prone to being timid or fearful of the new things he will encounter. Your pup's socialization began at the breeder's but now it is your responsibility to continue it. The socialization he receives up until the age of 12 weeks is the most critical, as this is the time when he forms his impressions of the outside world. Be especially careful during the eight-to-ten-week-old period, also known as the fear period. The interaction he receives during this time should be gentle and reassuring. Lack of socialization can manifest itself in fear and aggression as the dog grows up. He needs lots of human contact, affection, handling and exposure to other animals.

Once your pup has received his necessary vaccinations, feel free to take him out and about (on his lead, of course). Walk him around the neighborhood, take him on your daily errands, let people pet him, let him meet other dogs and pets, etc. Puppies do not have to try to make friends; there will be no shortage

Puppies love playtime with their owners, and energetic children will enjoy the company of an active Dobe puppy.

The breeder has carefully monitored the weight gain of your Doberman Pinscher puppy. If you provide a proper feeding and exercise regimen, your puppy will develop into a strong and healthy adult dog.

of people who will want to introduce themselves. Just make sure that you carefully supervise each meeting. If the neighborhood children want to say hello, for example, that is great—children and pups most often make great companions. Sometimes an excited child can unintentionally handle a pup too roughly, or an overzealous pup can playfully nip a little too hard. You want to make socialization experiences positive ones. What a pup learns during this very formative stage will affect his attitude toward future encounters. You want your dog to be comfortable around everyone. A pup that has a bad experience with a child may grow up to be a dog that is shy around or aggressive toward children.

CONSISTENCY IN TRAINING

Dogs, being pack animals, naturally need a leader, or else they try to establish dominance in their packs. When you bring a dog into your family, the choice of who becomes the leader and who becomes the "pack" is entirely up to you! Your pup's intuitive quest for dominance, coupled with the fact that it is nearly impossible to resist an adorable Doberman Pinscher pup, give the pup an almost unfair advantage in getting the upper hand! A pup will definitely test the waters to see what

IN DUE TIME

It will take at least two weeks for your puppy to become accustomed to his new surroundings. Give him lots of love, attention, handling, frequent opportunities to relieve himself, a diet he likes to eat and a place he can call his own.

he can and cannot do. Do not give in to those pleading eyes—stand your ground when it comes to disciplining the pup and make sure that all family members do the same. It will only confuse the pup when Mother tells him to get off the sofa when he is used to sitting up there with Father to watch the nightly news. Avoid discrepancies by having all members of the household decide on the rules before the pup even comes home...and be consistent in enforcing them! Early training shapes the dog's personality, so you cannot be unclear in what you expect.

PUPPY PROBLEMS

The majority of problems that are commonly seen in young pups will disappear as your dog gets older. However, how you deal with problems when he is young will determine how he reacts to discipline as an adult dog. It is important to establish who is boss (hopefully it will be you!) right away when you are first bonding with your dog. This bond will set the tone for the rest of your life together.

COMMON PUPPY PROBLEMS

The best way to prevent puppy problems is to be proactive in stopping an undesirable behavior as soon as it starts. The old saying "You can't teach an old dog new tricks" does not necessarily hold true, but it is true that it is much easier to discourage bad behavior in a young developing pup than to wait until the pup's bad behavior becomes the adult dog's bad habit. There are some problems that are especially prevalent in puppies as they develop.

NIPPING

As puppies start to teethe, they feel the need to sink their teeth into anything available... unfortunately that includes your fingers, arms, hair and toes. You may find this behavior cute for the first five seconds...until you feel just how sharp those puppy teeth are. This is something you want to discourage immediately and consistently with a firm "No!" (or whatever number of firm "Nos" it takes for him to understand that you mean business). Then replace your finger with an appropriate chew toy. While this behavior is merely

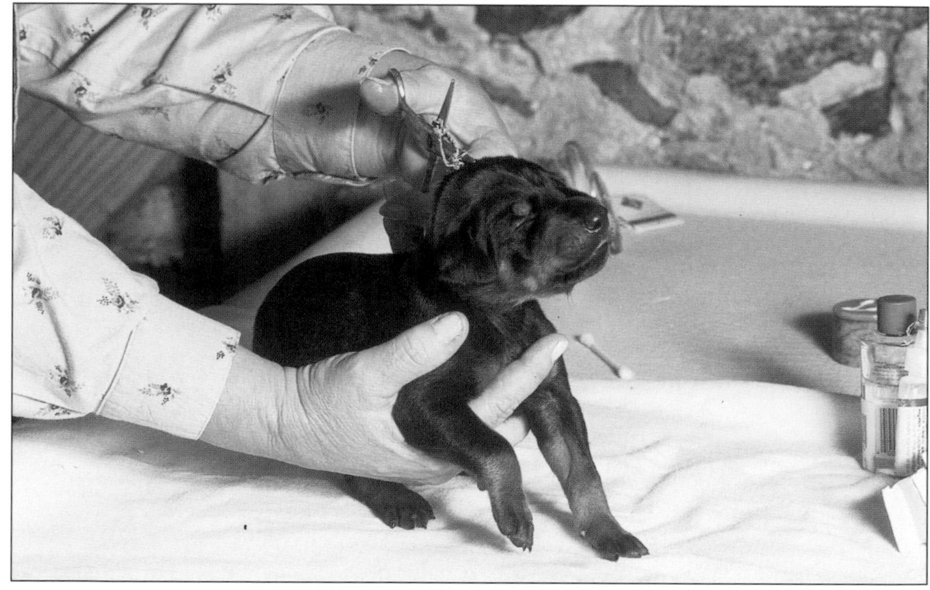

Ear cropping is usually done between two and five days old. It then takes four to six weeks of the pup's ears being set and taped in place for them to stand on their own.

Opposite page: The Doberman Pinscher comes in four acceptable colors, none of which is white. White Doberman Pinschers are frowned upon in show circles, though they make marvelous pets, provided their hearing and overall health have been suitably checked.

annoying when the dog is young, it can become dangerous as your Doberman Pinscher's adult teeth grow in and his jaws develop, and he continues to think it is okay to gnaw on human appendages. Your Doberman Pinscher does not mean any harm with a friendly nip, but he also does not know his own strength.

Crying/Whining

Your pup will often cry, whine, whimper, howl or make some type of commotion when he is left alone. This is basically his way of calling out for attention to make sure that you know he is there and that you have not forgotten about him. He feels insecure when he is left alone, when you are out of the house and he is in his crate or when you are in another part of the house and he cannot see you. The noise he is making is an expression of the anxiety he feels at being alone, so he needs to be taught that being alone is okay. You are not actually

PUP MEETS WORLD

Thorough socialization includes not only meeting new people but also being introduced to new experiences such as riding in the car, having his coat brushed, hearing the television, walking in a crowd—the list is endless. The more your pup experiences, and the more positive the experiences are, the less of a shock and the less frightening it will be for your pup to encounter new things.

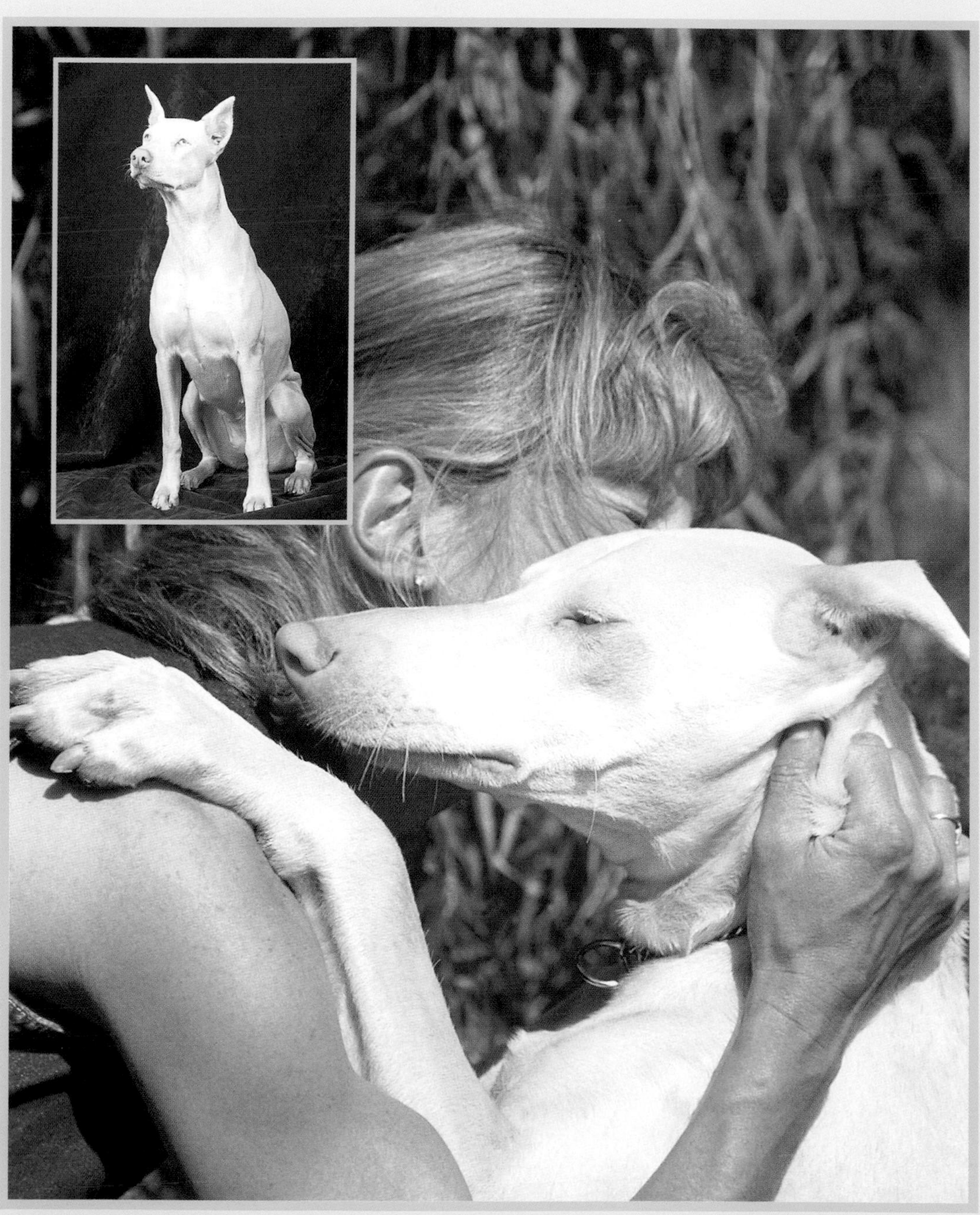

As puppies want to establish their position in the pack, they play-fight and roughhouse with their littermates.

training the dog to stop making noise; you are training him to feel comfortable when he is alone and thus removing the need for him to make the noise. This is where the crate with cozy bedding and a toy comes in handy. You want to know that he is safe when you are not there to supervise, and you know that he will be safe in his crate rather than roaming freely about the house. In order for the pup to stay in his crate without making a fuss, he needs to be comfortable in his crate. On that note, it is extremely important that the crate is never used as a form of punishment, or the pup will develop a negative association with the crate.

Accustom the pup to the crate in short, gradually increasing time intervals in which you put him in the crate, maybe with a treat, and stay in the room with him. If he cries or makes a fuss, do not go to him, but stay in his sight. Gradually he will realize that staying in his crate is okay without your help, and it will not be so traumatic for him when you are not around. You may want to leave the radio on softly when you leave the house; the sound of human voices may be comforting to him.

CHEWING TIPS

Chewing goes hand in hand with nipping in the sense that a teething puppy is always looking for a way to soothe his aching gums. In this case, instead of chewing on you, he may have taken a liking to your favorite shoe or something else that he should not be chewing. Again, realize that this is a normal canine behavior that does not need to be discouraged, only redirected. Your pup just needs to be taught what is acceptable to chew on and what is off-limits. Consistently tell him "No!" when you catch him chewing on something forbidden and give him a chew toy.

Conversely, praise him when you catch him chewing on something appropriate. In this way, you are discouraging the inappropriate behavior and reinforcing the desired behavior. The puppy's chewing should stop after his adult teeth have come in, but an adult dog continues to chew for various reasons—perhaps because he is bored, needs to relieve tension or just likes to chew. That is why it is important to redirect his chewing when he is still young.

As your Doberman Pinscher puppy matures, he will become more independent and less dependent on you, while still retaining his loyalty. This maturing pup has developed into a responsive and biddable companion.

For such a large breed, the Doberman Pinscher is relatively undemanding on his owner. He requires quality food, daily exercise and human contact.

EVERYDAY CARE OF YOUR DOBERMAN PINSCHER

DIETARY AND FEEDING CONSIDERATIONS

You have probably heard it a thousand times: "You are what you eat." Believe it or not, it's very true. Dogs are what you feed them because they have little choice in the matter. Even those people who truly want to feed their dogs the best often cannot do so because they do not know which foods are best for their dogs.

Dog foods are produced in three basic types: dry, semi-moist and canned. Dry foods are the choice of the cost-conscious because they are much less expensive than semi-moist and canned. Dry foods contain the least fat and the most preservatives. Most canned foods are 60–70% water, while semi-moist foods are so full of sugar that they are the least preferred by owners, though dogs welcome them (as a child does candy).

Three stages of development must be considered when selecting a diet for your dog: the puppy stage, the mid-age or adult stage and the senior stage.

TEST FOR PROPER DIET

A good test for proper diet is the color, odor and firmness of your dog's stool. A healthy dog usually produces three semi-hard stools per day. The stools should have no unpleasant odor. They should be the same color from excretion to excretion.

PUPPY DIETS

Puppies have a natural instinct to suck milk from their mother's teats. They exhibit this behavior from the first moments of their lives. If they don't suckle within a short while, the breeder attempts to put them onto their mother's nipples. A newborn's failure to suckle often requires that the breeder hand-feed the pup under the guidance of a veterinarian. This involves a baby bottle and a special formula. Their mother's milk is much better than any formula because it contains colostrum, a sort of antibiotic milk that protects the puppies during the first eight to ten weeks of their lives.

Puppies should be allowed to nurse for six weeks and they should be slowly weaned away

FOOD PREFERENCE

Selecting the best dry dog food is difficult. There is no majority consensus among veterinary scientists as to the value of nutrient analyses (protein, fat, fiber, moisture, ash, cholesterol, minerals, etc.). All agree that feeding trials are what matter most, but you also have to consider the individual dog. The dog's weight,

age and activity level, and what pleases his taste, all must be considered. It is probably best to take the advice of your veterinarian. Every dog's dietary requirements vary, even during the lifetime of a particular dog.

If your dog is fed a good dry food, he does not require supplements of meat or vegetables. Dogs do appreciate a little variety in their diets, so you may choose to stay with the same brand but vary the flavor. Alternatively, you may wish to add a little flavored stock to give a difference to the taste.

from their mother by alternating small portions of canned meat with their milk meals after they are about one month old. Then dry food is gradually added to the puppies' portions over the next few weeks.

By the time they are eight weeks old, they should be completely weaned and fed solely on quality puppy food. During this period, their diet is most important, as the puppy grows fastest during the first year of life.

Doberman Pinscher pups should be fed three meals per day when they are six to eight weeks of age. At eight weeks, the pup can be fed twice per day. Fussy eaters may require an additional smaller meal to maintain a good weight. Growth foods can be recommended by your veterinarian, and the puppy should be kept on this diet for up to 18 months.

Puppy diets should be complete and balanced for your dog's needs, and supplements of vitamins, minerals and protein should not be necessary.

Adult Diets

A dog is considered an adult when he has stopped growing in height and/or length. Do not consider the dog's weight when the decision is made to switch from a puppy diet to a maintenance diet. Again you should rely upon your veterinarian to recommend an acceptable maintenance diet. Major dog-food manufacturers specialize in this type of food and it is necessary for you to select the one best suited to your dog's needs. Active dogs may have different requirements than more sedate dogs. A Doberman Pinscher is fully mature around 12 months of age, though it often takes another 12 to 18 months for the dog to reach his peak as a performance animal.

Senior Diets

As dogs get older, their metabolism changes. The older dog usually exercises less, moves more slowly and sleeps more. This change in lifestyle and physiological performance requires a change in diet. Since these changes take place slowly, they might not be recognizable. What is easily recognizable is weight gain. By continually feeding your dog an adult-maintenance diet when he is slowing down metabolically, your dog will gain weight. Obesity in an older dog compounds the health problems that already accompany old age.

As your dog gets older, few of his organs function up to par. The kidneys slow down and the intestines become less efficient. These age-related factors are best handled with a change in diet and a change in feeding schedule to give smaller portions that are more easily digested.

There is no single best diet for every older dog. While many dogs do well on light or senior diets, other dogs do better on puppy

The Dobe puppy has a lot of growing to do! Discuss his diet with your breeder and vet to ensure the best nutrition for his development during this crucial stage.

STORING DOG FOOD

You must store your dry dog food carefully. Open packages of dog food quickly lose their vitamin value, usually within 90 days of being opened. Mold spores and vermin could also contaminate the food.

Doberman Pinschers, like all other dogs, would choose to eat human "junk food" over their dry food every day. Just as children would choose sweets over vegetables, your dog does not know what is good for him.

diets or other special premium diets such as lamb and rice. Be sensitive to your senior Doberman Pinscher's diet and this will help control other problems that may arise with your old friend.

WATER

Just as your dog needs proper nutrition from his food, water is an essential "nutrient" as well. Water keeps the dog's body properly hydrated and promotes normal function of the body's systems. During housebreaking it is necessary to keep an eye on how much water your Doberman Pinscher is drinking, but once he is reliably trained he should have access to clean fresh water at all times. Make sure that the dog's water bowl is clean, and change the water often.

EXERCISE

All dogs require some form of exercise, regardless of breed. A sedentary lifestyle is as harmful to a dog as it is to a person. The Doberman Pinscher happens to be an above-average active breed that requires more exercise than most breeds. Regular walks, play sessions in the yard and letting the dog run free in an enclosed area under your supervision are all sufficient forms of exercise for the Doberman Pinscher. For those who are more ambitious, you will find that your Doberman Pinscher will be able to keep up with you on extra-long walks or a morning run. Not only is exercise essential to keep the dog's body fit, it is essential to his mental well-being. A bored dog will find something

GRAIN-BASED DIETS

Some less expensive dog foods are based on grains and other plant proteins. While these products may appear to be attractively priced, many breeders prefer a diet based on animal proteins and believe that they are more conducive to your dog's health. Many grain-based diets rely on soy protein, which may cause flatulence (passing gas).

There are many cases, however, when your dog might require a special diet. These special requirements should only be recommended by your veterinarian.

The Doberman Pinscher will welcome a securely fenced area in which to run freely, expending some of his considerable energy and keeping his body fit.

Meals for puppies can be a "splashing" fun time. Be sure your puppy drinks as well as plays in his water bowl.

to do, which often manifests itself in some type of destructive behavior. In this sense, exercise is essential for the owner's mental well-being as well!

GROOMING

BRUSHING

A natural bristle brush or a hound glove can be used for regular routine brushing. Daily brushing is effective for removing dead hair and stimulating the dog's natural oils to add shine and a healthy look to the coat. Although the Doberman Pinscher's coat is short and close, it does require a five-minute once-over to keep it looking its shiny best. Regular grooming sessions are also a good way to spend time with your dog. Many dogs grow to like the feel of being brushed and will enjoy the daily routine.

BATHING

Dogs do not need to be bathed as often as humans, but bathing as needed is essential for healthy skin and a healthy, shiny coat. Again, like most anything, if you accustom your Doberman Pinscher to being bathed as a puppy, it will be second nature by the time he grows up. You want your dog to be at ease in the bath or else it could end up a wet, soapy, messy ordeal for both of you!

Brush your Doberman Pinscher thoroughly before

FEEDING TIPS

- Dog food must be at room temperature, neither too hot nor too cold. Fresh water, changed daily and served in a clean bowl, is mandatory, especially when feeding dry food.
- Never feed your dog from the table while you are eating, and never feed your dog leftovers from your own meal. They usually contain too much fat and too much seasoning.
- Dogs must chew their food. Hard pellets are excellent; soups and stews are to be avoided. Don't add any extras to normal dog food, as it is usually balanced, and adding something extra destroys the balance.
- Except for age-related changes, dogs do not require dietary variations. They can be fed the same diet, day after day, without becoming bored or ill.

wetting his coat. Make sure that your dog has a good non-slip surface to stand on. Begin by wetting the dog's coat. A shower or hose attachment is necessary for thoroughly wetting and rinsing the coat. Check the water temperature to make sure that it is neither too hot nor too cold.

Next, apply shampoo to the dog's coat and work it into a good lather. You should purchase a shampoo that is made for dogs. Do not use a product made for human hair. Wash the head last; you do not want shampoo to drip into the dog's eyes while you are washing the rest of his body. Work the shampoo all the way down to the skin. You can use this

GROOMING EQUIPMENT

How much grooming equipment you purchase will depend on how much grooming you are going to do. Here are some basics:

- Natural bristle brush
- Grooming glove
- Flea comb
- Scissors
- Blow dryer
- Rubber mat
- Dog shampoo
- Spray hose attachment
- Towels
- Ear cleaner
- Cotton balls
- Nail clippers

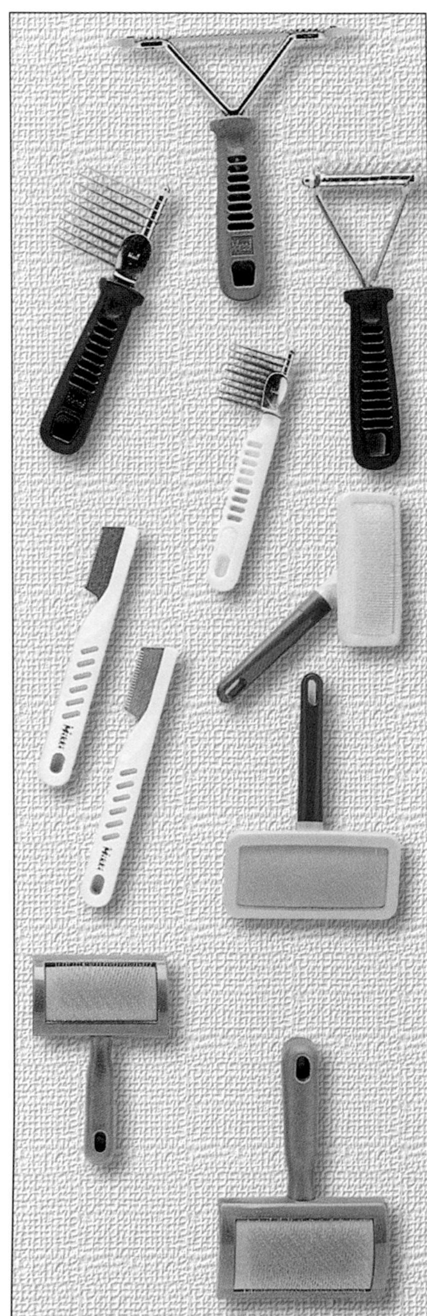

Photo courtesy of Mikki Pet Products.

Your local pet shop will have a wide variety of brushes, combs and other grooming tools necessary to keep your Doberman Pinscher's coat in good condition.

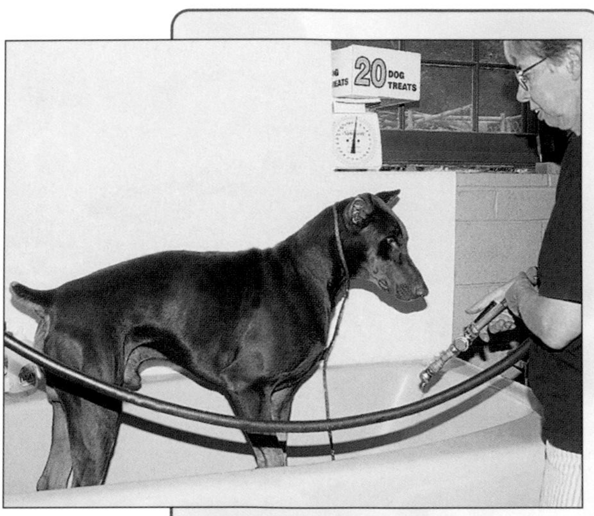

BATHING BEAUTY

Once you are sure that the dog is thoroughly rinsed, squeeze the excess water out of his coat with your hand and dry him with a heavy towel. You can then let the coat air-dry on its own, making sure the dog does not become chilled. In cold weather, never allow your dog outside with a damp coat.

There are "dry bath" products on the market, which are sprays and powders intended for spot cleaning, that can be used between regular baths if necessary. They are not substitutes for regular baths, but they are easy to use for touch-ups as they do not require rinsing.

opportunity to check the skin for any bumps, bites or other abnormalities. Do not neglect any area of the body—get all of the hard-to-reach places.

Once the dog has been thoroughly shampooed, he requires an equally thorough rinsing. Shampoo left in the coat can be irritating to the skin. Protect his eyes from the shampoo by shielding them with your hand and directing the flow of water in the opposite direction. You should also avoid getting water in the ear canal. Be prepared for your dog to shake out his coat—you might want to stand back, but make sure you have a hold on the dog to keep him from running through the house.

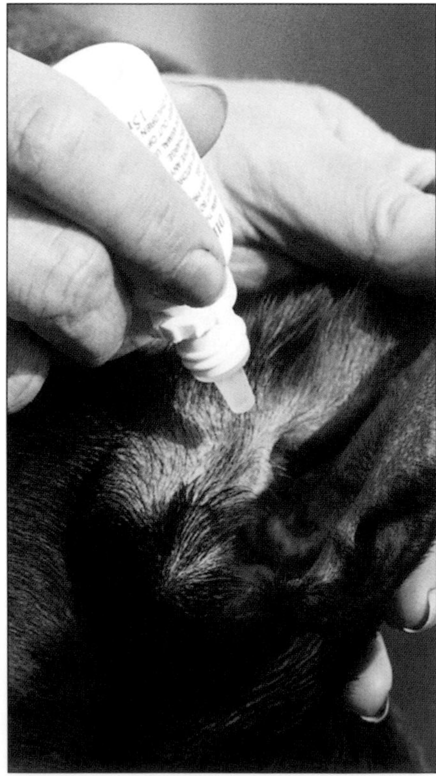

Your local pet shop will have a special product, either in liquid or powder form, to assist you in keeping your Doberman Pinscher's ears clean and free of debris.

Ear Cleaning

The ears should be kept clean and any excess hair inside the ear should be trimmed. Ears can be cleaned with a cotton ball and special cleaner or ear powder made especially for dogs. Be on the lookout for any signs of infection or ear-mite infestation. If your Doberman Pinscher has been shaking his head or scratching at his ears frequently, this usually indicates a problem. If his ears have an unusual odor, this is a sure sign of mite infestation or infection, and a signal to have his ears checked by the vet.

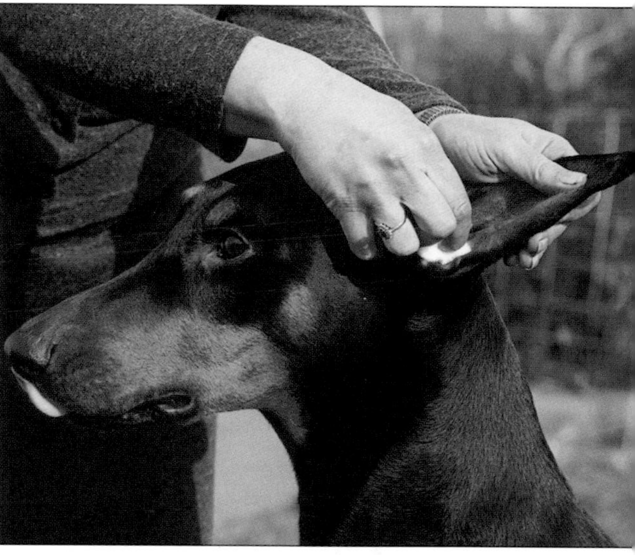

Use a cotton ball to assist in keeping your Doberman Pinscher's ears clean. Examine the ears for ear mites. If you find any, contact your vet immediately.

Nail Clipping

Your Doberman Pinscher should be accustomed to having his nails trimmed at an early age, since it will be part of your maintenance routine throughout his life. Not only does it look nicer, but a dog with long nails can cause injury if he scratches someone unintentionally. Also, a long nail has a better chance of ripping and bleeding, or causing the feet to spread. A good rule of thumb is that if you can hear your dog's nails clicking on the floor when he walks, his nails are too long.

Before you start cutting, make sure you can identify the "quick" in each nail. The quick is a blood vessel that runs through the center of each nail and grows rather close to the end. It will bleed if accidentally cut, which will be quite painful for the dog as it contains nerve endings. Keep some type of clotting agent on hand, such as a styptic pencil or styptic powder (the type used for shaving). This will stop the bleeding quickly when applied to the end of the cut nail. Do not panic if

SOAP IT UP

The use of human soap products like shampoo, bubble bath and hand soap can be damaging to a dog's coat and skin. Human products are too strong; they remove the protective oils coating the dog's hair and skin that make him water-resistant. Use only shampoo made especially for dogs. You may like to use a medicated shampoo, which will help to keep external parasites at bay.

Use a nail clipper made especially for dogs. Start trimming your dog's nails at an early age so he will be accustomed to this routine.

With black or dark nails, where the quick is not easy to see, it's best to clip only the tip of the nail or to use a file.

In light-colored nails, clipping is much simpler because you can see the vein (or quick) that grows inside the casing.

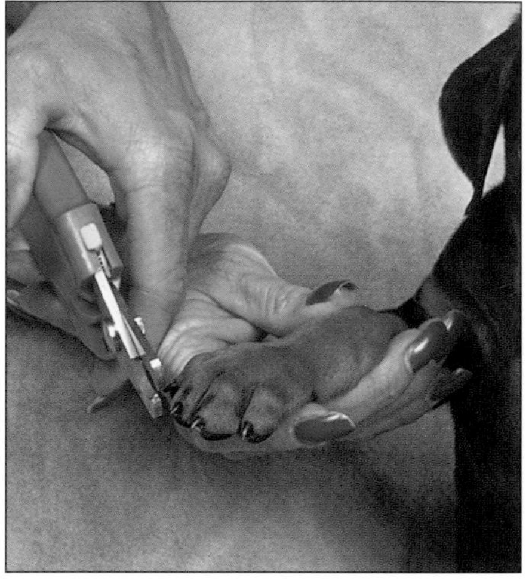

you cut the quick, just stop the bleeding and talk soothingly to your dog. Once he has calmed down, move on to the next nail. It is better to clip a little at a time, particularly with black-nailed dogs.

PEDICURE TIP

A dog that spends a lot of time outside on a hard surface, such as cement or pavement, will have his nails naturally worn down and may not need to have them trimmed as often, except maybe in the colder months when he is not outside as much. Regardless, it is best to get your dog accustomed to the nail-trimming procedure at an early age so that he is used to it. Some dogs are especially sensitive about having their feet touched, but if a dog has experienced it since puppyhood, it should not bother him.

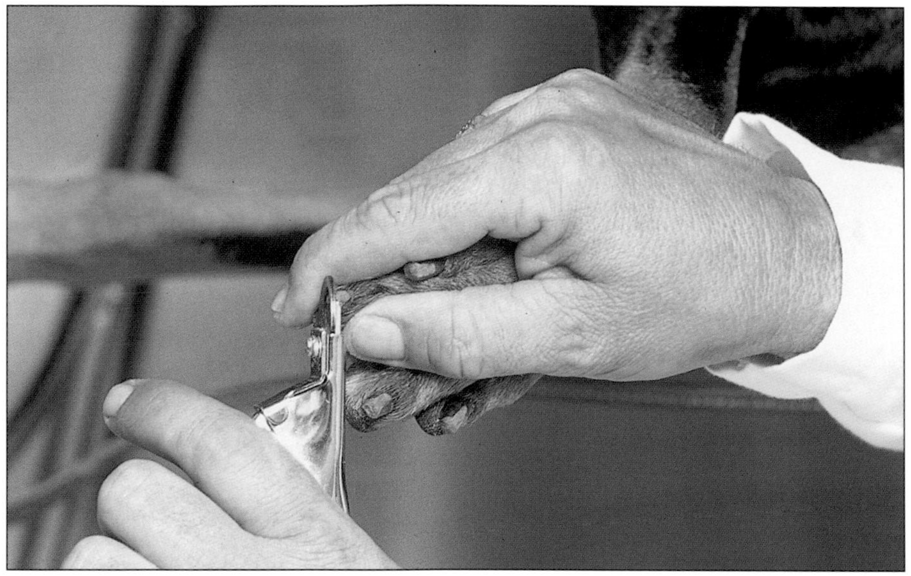

There are different types of dog nail clippers. The guillotine-type, shown here, works much like its namesake, as you insert the nail into the opening and the clipper lowers to take off the end of the nail.

Hold your pup steady as you begin trimming his nails; you do not want him to make any sudden movements or run away. Talk to him soothingly and stroke him as you clip. Holding his foot in your hand, simply take off the end of each nail in one quick clip. You can purchase nail clippers that are specially made for dogs; you can probably find them wherever you buy pet supplies.

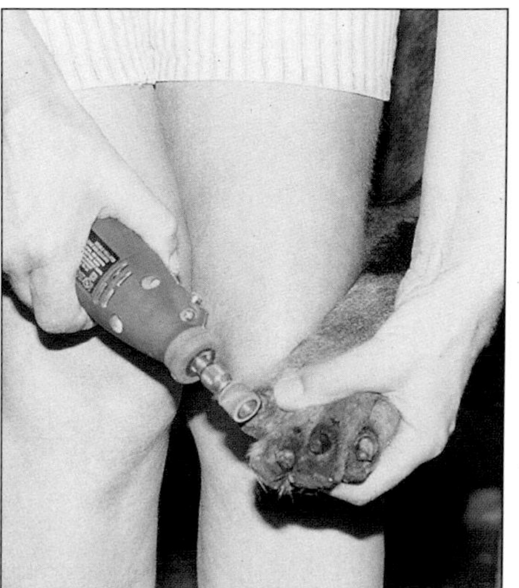

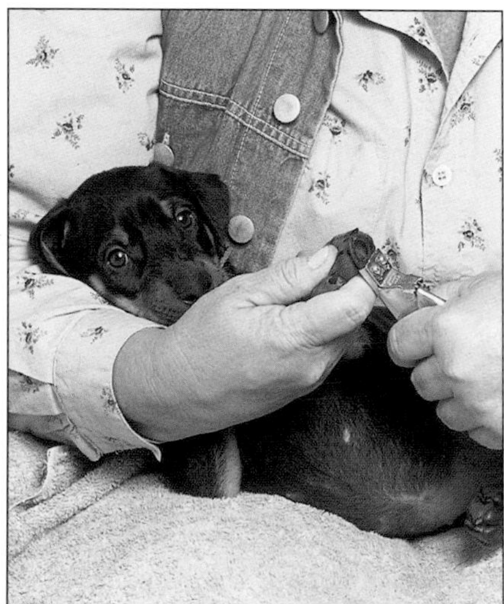

Left: Electrically driven grinders are used by professional groomers to keep dogs' nails at their proper length. Right: You won't need very strong clippers to cut a puppy's nails.

TRAVEL TIP

Never leave your dog alone in the car. In hot weather, your dog can die from the high temperature inside a closed vehicle; even a car parked in the shade can heat up very quickly. Leaving the window open is dangerous as well since the dog can hurt himself trying to get out.

TRAVELING WITH YOUR DOG

Car Travel

You should accustom your Doberman Pinscher to riding in a car at an early age. You may or may not take him in the car often, but at the very least he will need to go to the vet and you do not want these trips to be traumatic for the dog or troublesome for you. The safest way for a dog to ride in the car is in his crate.

Put the pup in the crate and see how he reacts. If he seems uneasy, you can have a passenger hold him on his lap while you drive. Of course, this solution will only work when your Doberman Pinscher is a puppy! Another option is a specially made safety harness for dogs, which straps the dog in much like a seat belt. If you have a station wagon, sports utility or similar vehicle, you can partition the rear section of your vehicle to create a secure area. Do not let the dog roam loose in the vehicle—this is very dangerous! If you should stop short, your dog can be thrown and injured. If the dog starts climbing on you and pestering you while you are driving, you will not be able to concentrate on the road. It is an unsafe situation for everyone—human and canine.

For long trips, be prepared to stop to let the dog relieve himself. Bring along whatever you need to clean up after him. You should also bring along some paper towels and old rags, should he have an accident in the car or become carsick.

Air Travel

Contact your chosen airline before proceeding with your travel plans that include your Doberman Pinscher. The dog will be required to travel in a fiberglass crate and you should always check in advance with the airline regarding specific requirements for the crate's size, type and labeling.

To help put the dog at ease, give him one of his favorite toys in the crate. Do not feed the dog for several hours prior to checking in so that you minimize his need to relieve himself. However, some airlines require that the dog must be fed within four hours of arriving at the airport, in which case a light meal is best. For long trips, you will have to attach food and water bowls to the outside the dog's crate so that airline employees can tend to him between legs of the trip.

Make sure that your dog is properly identified and that your contact information appears on his ID tags and on his crate. Your Doberman will travel in a different area of the plane than the human passengers, so every rule

ON THE ROAD

If you are going on a long road trip with your dog, be sure the hotels are dog-friendly. Many hotels do not accept dogs. Also take along some ice that can be thawed and offered to your dog if he becomes overheated. Most dogs like to lick ice.

Never drive with your Doberman Pinscher(s) loose inside your car. If you bring your dog along with you when driving, secure him with a suitable wire barrier, as shown here, or in a portable crate.

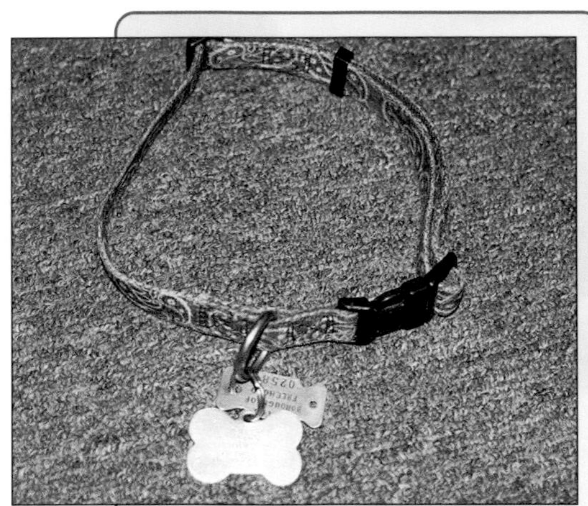

COLLAR REQUIRED

If your dog gets lost, he is not able to ask for directions home. Identification tags fastened to the collar give important information—the dog's name, the owner's name, the owner's address and a telephone number where the owner can be reached. This makes it easy for whoever finds the dog to contact the owner and arrange to have the dog returned. An added advantage is that a person will be more likely to approach a lost dog who has ID tags on his collar; it tells the person that this is somebody's pet rather than a stray. This is the easiest and fastest method of identification, provided that the tags stay on the collar and the collar stays on the dog.

must be strictly followed to prevent the risk of getting separated from your dog. Be comforted by the fact that transporting pets is a rather routine procedure for most major airlines.

To help the dog be at ease, put one of his favorite toys in the crate with him. Do not feed the dog for at least six hours before the trip to minimize his need to relieve himself. However, certain regulations specify that water must always be made available to the dog in the crate.

BOARDING

So you want to take a family vacation—and you want to include *all* members of the family. You would probably make arrangements for accommodations ahead of time anyway, but this is especially important when traveling with a dog. You do not want to make an overnight stop at the only place around for miles and find out that they do not allow dogs. Also, you do not want to reserve a place for your family without confirming that you are traveling with a dog because, if it is against the hotel's policy, you may not have a place to stay.

Alternatively, if you are traveling and choose not to bring your Doberman Pinscher, you will have to make arrangements for him while you are away. Some options are to bring him to a neighbor's house to stay while you are gone, to have a trusted neighbor drop by often or stay at your house or to bring your dog to a reputable boarding kennel. If you choose to board him at a kennel, you should stop by to see the facilities

GOING ABROAD

For international travel, you will have to make arrangements well in advance (perhaps months), as countries' regulations pertaining to bringing in animals differ. There may be special health certificates and/or vaccinations that your dog will need before taking the trip; sometimes this has to be done within a certain time frame. When traveling to rabies-free countries, you will need to bring proof of the dog's rabies vaccination and there will likely be a quarantine period upon arrival.

provided and where the dogs are kept to make sure that it is clean. Talk to some of the employees and see how they treat the dogs—do they spend time with the dogs, play with them, exercise them, etc.? You know that your Doberman Pinscher will not be happy unless he gets regular activity. Also find out the kennel's policy on vaccinations and what they require. This is for all of the dogs' safety, since when dogs are kept together, there is a greater risk of diseases being passed from dog to dog. Many veterinarians offer boarding facilities; this is another option.

IDENTIFICATION

Your Doberman Pinscher is your valued companion and friend. That is why you always keep a close eye on him and you have made sure that he cannot escape from the yard or wriggle out of his collar and run away from you. However, accidents can happen and there may come a time when your dog unexpectedly gets separated from you. If this unfortunate event should occur, the first thing on your mind will be finding him. Proper identification, including an ID tag, and possibly a tattoo and/or microchip, will increase the chances of his being returned to you safely and quickly.

If you are fortunate enough to have a friend to "dogsit" your Doberman Pinscher, he will be happier in a family environment and should make himself comfortable in your friend's home.

TRAINING YOUR
DOBERMAN PINSCHER

Living with an untrained dog is a lot like owning a piano that you do not know how to play—it is a nice object to look at but it does not do much more than that to bring you pleasure. Now try taking piano lessons and suddenly the piano comes alive and brings forth magical sounds and rhythms that set your heart singing and your body swaying.

The same is true with your Doberman Pinscher. At first you enjoy seeing him around the house. He does not do much with you other than to need food, water and exercise. Come to think of it, he does not bring you much joy, either. He is a big responsibility with a very small return. Often he develops unacceptable behaviors that annoy you, to say nothing of bad habits that may end up costing you great sums of money. Not a good thing!

Now train your Doberman Pinscher. Enroll in an obedience class. Teach him good manners as you learn how and why he behaves the way he does. Find out how to communicate with your dog and how to recognize and understand his communications with you. Suddenly the dog takes on a new role in your life—he is clever, interesting, well behaved and fun to be with. He demonstrates his bond of devotion to you daily. In other words, your Doberman Pinscher does wonders for your ego because he constantly

PARENTAL GUIDANCE

Training a dog is a life experience. Many parents admit that much of what they know about raising children they learned from caring for their dogs. Dogs respond to love, fairness and guidance, just as children do. Become a good dog owner and you may become an even better parent.

reminds you that you are not only his leader, you are his hero! Miraculous things have happened—you have a wonderful dog (even your family and friends have noticed the transformation!) and you feel good about yourself.

Those involved with teaching dog obedience and counseling owners about their dogs' behavior have discovered some interesting facts about dog ownership. For example, training dogs when they are puppies results in the highest rate of success in developing well-mannered and well-adjusted adult dogs. Training an older dog, from six months to six years of age, can produce almost equal results, providing that the owner accepts the dog's slower rate of learning capability and is willing to work patiently to help the dog succeed at developing to his fullest potential. Unfortunately, many owners of untrained adult dogs lack the patience factor, so they do not persist until their dogs are successful at learning particular behaviors.

Training a puppy age 8 to 16 weeks (20 weeks at the most) is like working with a dry sponge in a pool of water. The pup soaks up whatever you show him and constantly looks for more things to do and learn. At this early age, his body is not yet producing hormones, and therein lies the reason for such a high rate of success. Without hormones, he is focused on his owners and not particularly interested in investigating other places, dogs, people, etc. You are his leader: his provider of food, water, shelter and security. He latches onto you and wants to stay close. He will usually follow you from room to room, will not let you out of his sight when you are outdoors with him and will respond in like manner to the people and animals you encounter. If you greet a friend warmly, he will be happy to greet the person

REAP THE REWARDS

If you start with a normal, healthy dog and give him time, patience and some carefully executed lessons, you will reap the rewards of that training for the life of the dog. And what a life it will be! The two of you will find immeasurable pleasure in the companionship you have built together with love, respect and understanding.

PLAN TO PLAY

Your Dobe should also have regular play and exercise sessions when he is with you or a family member. Exercise for a very young puppy can consist of a short walk around the house or yard. Playing can include fetching games with a large ball or a special toy. (All puppies teethe and need soft things upon which to chew.) Remember to restrict play periods to indoors within his living area (the family room, for example) until he is completely house-trained.

as well. If, however, you are hesitant or anxious about the approach of a stranger, he will respond accordingly.

Once the puppy begins to produce hormones, his natural curiosity emerges and he begins to investigate the world around him. It is at this time when you may notice that the untrained dog begins to wander away from you and even ignore your commands to stay close. When his behavior becomes a problem, the owner has two choices: get rid of the dog or train him. It is strongly urged that you choose the latter option.

Occasionally there are no classes available within a reasonable distance from the owner's home. Sometimes there are classes available, but the tuition is too costly. Whatever the circumstances, the solution to training your Doberman without formal

Conscientious breeders keep the puppies' quarters as spotless as possible, never allowing the pups to remain near their droppings.

obedience classes lies within the pages of this book. This chapter is devoted to helping you train your Doberman Pinscher at home. If the recommended procedures are followed faithfully, you may expect positive results that will prove rewarding both to you and your dog.

Whether your new charge is a puppy or a mature adult, the methods of teaching and the techniques we use in training basic behaviors are the same. After all, no dog, whether puppy or adult, likes harsh or inhumane methods. All creatures, however, respond favorably to gentle motivational methods and sincere praise and encouragement. Now let us get started.

HIS OWN LITTLE CORNER

Mealtime should be a peaceful time for your puppy. Do not put his food and water bowls in a high-traffic area in the house. For example, give him his own little corner of the kitchen where

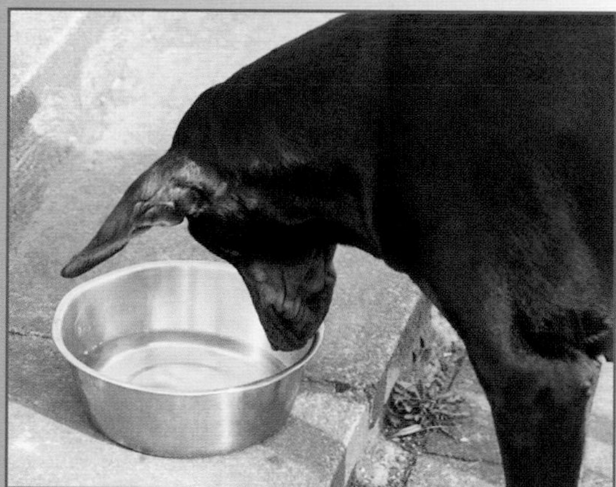

he can eat undisturbed and where he will not be underfoot. Do not allow small children or other family members to disturb the pup when he is eating.

HOUSEBREAKING

You can train a puppy to relieve himself wherever you choose, but this must be somewhere suitable. You should bear in mind from the outset that when your puppy is old enough to go out in public places, any canine deposits must be removed at once. You will always have to carry with you a small plastic bag or "poop-scoop."

Outdoor training includes such surfaces as grass, soil or earth and cement. Indoor training usually means training your dog to newspaper; not a viable option for a Dobe owner! When deciding on the surface and location that you will want your Doberman Pinscher to use, be sure it is going to be permanent. Training your dog to grass and then changing your mind two months later is extremely difficult for both dog and owner.

Next, choose the command you will use each and every time you want your puppy to void. "Be quick" and "Hurry up" are examples of commands commonly used by dog owners. Get in the habit of giving the puppy your chosen relief command before

TAKE THE LEAD

Do not carry your dog to his relief area. Lead him there on a leash or, better yet, encourage him to follow you to the spot. If you start carrying him to his spot, you might end up doing this routine forever and your dog will have the satisfaction of having trained *you.*

you take him out. That way, when he becomes an adult, you will be able to determine if he wants to go out when you ask him. A confirmation will be signs of interest, such as wagging his tail, watching you intently, going to the door, etc.

Puppy's Needs

The puppy needs to relieve himself after play periods, after each meal, after he has been sleeping and any time he indicates that he is looking for a place to urinate or defecate.

The urinary and intestinal tract muscles of very young puppies are not fully developed. Therefore, like human babies, puppies need to relieve themselves frequently. Take your puppy out often—every hour for an eight-week-old, for example. The older the puppy, the less often he will need to relieve himself. Finally, as a mature healthy adult, he will require only three to five relief trips per day.

Housing

Since the type of housing and control you provide for your puppy has a direct relationship on the success of house-training, we consider the various aspects of both before we begin training.

Bringing a new puppy home and turning him loose in your house can be compared to turning a child loose in a sports arena and

CANINE DEVELOPMENT SCHEDULE

It is important to understand how and at what age a puppy develops into adulthood. If you are a puppy owner, consult the following Canine Development Schedule to determine the stage of development your puppy is currently experiencing. This knowledge will help you as you work with the puppy in the weeks and months ahead.

Period	Age	Characteristics
First to Third	Birth to Seven Weeks	Puppy needs food, sleep and warmth, and responds to simple and gentle touching. Needs mother for security and disciplining. Needs littermates for learning and interacting with other dogs. Pup learns to function within a pack and learns pack order of dominance. Begin socializing with adults and children for short periods. Begins to become aware of his environment.
Fourth	Eight to Twelve Weeks	Brain is fully developed. Needs socializing with outside world. Remove from mother and littermates. Needs to change from canine pack to human pack. Human dominance necessary. Fear period occurs between 8 and 16 weeks. Avoid fright and pain.
Fifth	Thirteen to Sixteen Weeks	Training and formal obedience should begin. Less association with other dogs, more with people, places, situations. Period will pass easily if you remember this is pup's change-to-adolescence time. Be firm and fair. Flight instinct prominent. Permissiveness and over-disciplining can do permanent damage. Praise for good behavior.
Juvenile	Four to Eight Months	Another fear period about 7 to 8 months of age. It passes quickly, but be cautious of fright and pain. Sexual maturity reached. Dominant traits established. Dog should understand sit, down, come and stay by now.

Note: These are approximate time frames. Allow for individual differences in puppies.

ATTENTION!
Your dog is actually training you at the same time you are training him. Dogs do things to get attention. They usually repeat whatever succeeds in getting your attention.

telling the child that the place is all his! The sheer enormity of the place would be too much for him to handle.

Instead, offer the puppy clearly defined areas where he can play, sleep, eat and live. A room of the house where the family gathers is the most obvious choice. Puppies are social animals and need to feel a part of the pack right from the start. Hearing your voice, watching you while you are doing things and smelling you nearby are all positive reinforcers that he is now a member of your pack. Usually a family room, the kitchen or a nearby adjoining breakfast area is ideal for providing safety and security for both puppy and owner.

Within that room, there should be a smaller area that the puppy can call his own. An alcove, a wire or fiberglass dog crate or a partitioned (not boarded!) corner from which he can view the activities of his new family will be fine. The size of the area or crate is the key factor here. The area must be large enough for the puppy to lie down and stretch out as well as stand up without rubbing his head on the top, yet small enough so that he cannot relieve himself at one end and sleep at the other without coming into contact with his droppings.

The designated area should include clean bedding and a toy. Water must always be available, in a non-spill container, although, during house-training, you will need to be aware of when your pup eats and drinks so you can take him out accordingly. Dogs are, by nature, clean animals and will not remain close to their relief areas unless forced to do so. In those cases, they then become dirty dogs and usually remain that way for life.

Control

By *control*, we mean helping the puppy to create a lifestyle pattern that will be compatible to that of his human pack (*you*!). Just as we guide little children to learn our way of life, we must show the puppy when it is time to play, eat, sleep, exercise and even entertain himself.

Your puppy should always sleep in his crate. He should also learn that, during times of household confusion and excessive human activity such as at breakfast when family members are preparing for the day, he can play by himself in safety and comfort in his crate. Each time you leave the puppy alone, he should be crated. Puppies are chewers. They cannot tell the difference between lamp cords, television wires, shoes, table legs, etc. Chewing into a television wire, for example, can be fatal to the puppy, while a shorted wire can start a fire in the house. Crating the pup prevents these potential dangers.

If the puppy chews the arm of the chair when he is alone, you will probably discipline him angrily when you get home. Thus, he makes the association that your coming home means he is going to punished. (He will not remember chewing the chair and is incapable of making the association of the discipline with his naughty deed.) Again, the crate prevents the pup from getting into trouble.

READ THE HEADLINES!

Never line your pup's sleeping area with newspaper. Puppy litters are usually raised on newspaper and, once in your home, the puppy will immediately associate newspaper with voiding. Never put newspaper on any floor while house-training, as this will only confuse the puppy. Finally, restrict water intake after evening meals. Offer a few licks at a time—never let a young puppy gulp water after meals.

Contending with a new set of ears, potty lessons and obedience training can be overwhelming for the young Dobe.

Other times of excitement, such as visits from friends, family parties, etc., can be fun for the puppy, providing he can view the activities from the security of his crate. He is not underfoot and he is not being fed all sorts of tidbits that will probably cause him stomach distress, yet he still feels a part of the fun.

Schedule

A puppy should be taken to his relief area each time he is released

As your Dobe puppy grows in size, he also grows in strength and power. Training from an early age ensures that you will always be in control of your dog.

GOLDEN RULE

The golden rule of dog training is simple. For each "question" (command), there is only one correct answer (reaction). One command = one reaction. Keep practicing the command until the dog reacts correctly without hesitating. Be repetitive but not monotonous. Dogs get bored just as people do!

from his crate, after meals, after play sessions, when he first awakens in the morning (at age eight weeks, this can mean 5 a.m.!). The puppy will indicate that he's ready "to go" by circling or sniffing busily—do not misinterpret these signs. For a puppy less than ten weeks of age, a routine of taking him out every hour is necessary. As the puppy grows, he will be able to wait for longer periods of time.

Keep trips to his relief area short. Stay no more than five or six minutes and then return to the house. If he goes during that

time, praise him lavishly and take him indoors immediately. If he does not, but he has an accident when you go back indoors, pick him up immediately, say "No! No!" and return to his relief area. Wait a few minutes, then return to the house again. Never hit a puppy or put his face in urine or excrement when he has had an accident!

Once indoors, put the puppy in his crate until you clean up his accident, then release him to the family area and watch him more closely than before. Chances are, his accident was a result of your not picking up his signal or waiting too long before offering him the opportunity to relieve himself. Never hold a grudge against the puppy for accidents. Let the puppy learn that going outdoors means it is time to relieve himself, not play. Once trained, he will be able to play indoors and out and still differentiate between the times for play versus the times for relief.

Help the pup develop regular hours for naps, being alone, playing by himself and just resting, all in his crate. Encourage him to entertain himself while you are busy with your activities. Let him learn that having you near is comforting, but it is not your main purpose in life to provide him with undivided attention.

Each time you put your puppy in his own area, use the same command, whatever suits best. Soon, he will run to his crate or special area when he hears you say those words.

Crate training provides safety for you, the puppy and the home. It also provides the puppy with a feeling of security, and that helps the puppy achieve self-confidence and clean habits. Remember that one of the primary ingredients in house-training your puppy is control. Regardless of your

HOW MANY TIMES A DAY?

AGE	RELIEF TRIPS
To 14 weeks	10
14–22 weeks	8
22–32 weeks	6
Adulthood (dog stops growing)	4

These are estimates, of course, but they are a guide to the *minimum* number of opportunities a dog should have each day to relieve himself.

lifestyle, there will always be occasions when you will need to have a place where your dog can stay and be happy and safe. Crate training is the answer for now and in the future.

In conclusion, a few key elements are really all you need for a successful house-training method—consistency, frequency, praise, control and supervision. By following these procedures with a normal, healthy puppy, you and the

THE SUCCESS METHOD

Success that comes by luck is usually short-lived. Success that comes by well-thought-out proven methods is often more easily achieved and permanent. This is the Success Method. It is designed to give you, the puppy owner, a simple yet proven way to help your puppy develop clean living habits and a feeling of security in his new environment.

6 Steps to Successful Crate Training

1 Tell the puppy "Crate time!" and place him in the crate with a small treat (a piece of cheese or half of a biscuit). Let him stay in the crate for five minutes while you are in the same room. Then release him and praise lavishly. Never release him when he is fussing. Wait until he is quiet before you let him out.

2 Repeat Step 1 several times a day.

3 The next day, place the puppy in the crate as before. Let him stay there for ten minutes. Do this several times.

4 Continue building time in five-minute increments until the puppy stays in his crate for 30 minutes with you in the room. Always take him to his relief area after prolonged periods in his crate.

5 Now go back to Step 1 and let the puppy stay in his crate for five minutes, this time while you are out of the room.

6 Once again, build crate time in five-minute increments with you out of the room. When the puppy will stay willingly in his crate (he may even fall asleep!) for 30 minutes with you out of the room, he will be ready to stay in it for several hours at a time.

THE CLEAN LIFE

By providing sleeping and resting quarters that fit the dog, and offering frequent opportunities to relieve himself outside his quarters, the puppy quickly learns that the outdoors is the place to go when he needs to urinate or defecate. It also reinforces his innate desire to keep his sleeping quarters clean. This, in turn, helps develop the muscle control that will eventually produce a dog with clean living habits.

puppy will soon be past the stage of accidents and ready to move on to a full and rewarding life together.

ROLES OF DISCIPLINE, REWARD AND PUNISHMENT

Discipline, training one to act in accordance with rules, brings order to life. It is as simple as that. Without discipline, particularly in a group society, chaos reigns supreme and the group will eventually perish. Humans and canines are social animals and need some form of discipline in order to function effectively. They must procure food, protect their home base and their young and reproduce to keep the species going.

If there were no discipline in the lives of social animals, they would eventually die from starvation and/or predation by other stronger animals. In the case of domestic canines, dogs need discipline in their lives in order to understand how their pack (you and other family members) functions and how they must act in order to survive.

A large humane society in a highly populated area recently surveyed dog owners regarding

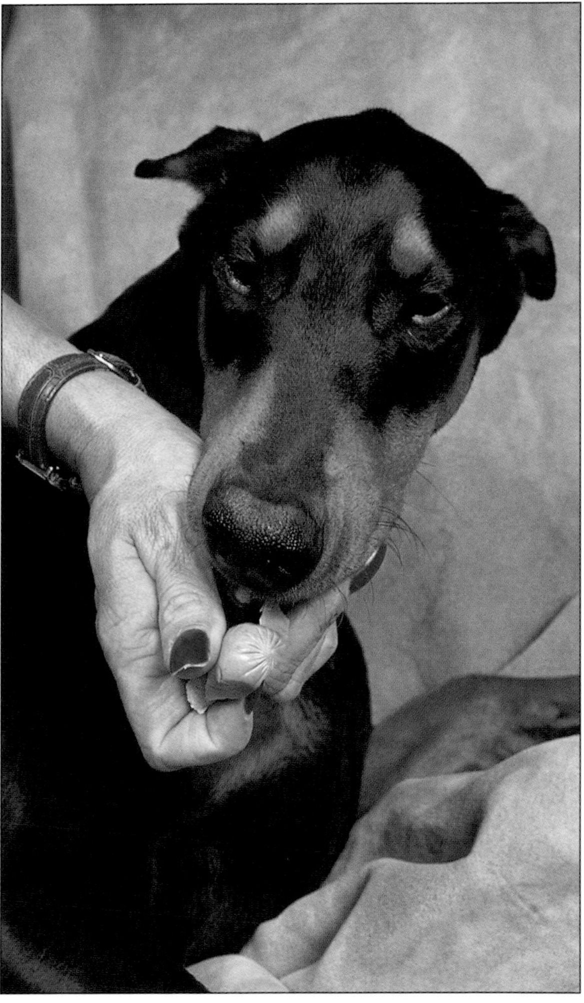

A tasty treat is every Doberman's choice reward, especially if seasoned with a dash of praise.

TRAINING RULES

If you want to be successful in training your dog, you have four rules to obey yourself:

1. Develop an understanding of how a dog thinks.
2. Do not blame the dog for lack of communication.
3. Define your dog's personality and act accordingly.
4. Have patience and be consistent.

their satisfaction with their relationships with their dogs. People who had trained their dogs were 75% more satisfied with their pets than those who had never trained their dogs.

Dr. Edward Thorndike, a noted psychologist, established *Thorndike's Theory of Learning,* which states that a behavior that results in a pleasant event tends to be repeated. Likewise, a behavior that results in an unpleasant event tends not to be repeated. It is this theory on which training methods are based today. For example, if you manipulate a dog to perform a specific behavior and reward him for doing it, he is likely to do it again because he enjoyed the end result.

Occasionally, punishment, a penalty inflicted for an offense, is necessary. The best type of punishment often comes from an outside source. For example, a child is told not to touch the stove because he may get burned. He disobeys and touches the stove. In doing so, he receives a burn. From that time on, he respects the heat of the stove and avoids contact with it. Therefore, a behavior that results in an unpleasant event tends not to be repeated.

A good example of a dog's learning the hard way is the dog who chases the house cat. He is told many times to leave the cat alone, yet he persists in teasing the cat. Then one day he begins chasing the cat but the cat turns and swipes a claw across the dog's face, leaving him with a painful gash on his nose. The result is that the dog stops chasing the cat.

TRAINING EQUIPMENT

Collar and Leash

For a Doberman Pinscher, the collar and leash that you use for training must be one with which you are easily able to work, not too heavy for the dog and perfectly safe.

Treats

Have a bag of treats on hand. Something nutritious and easy to swallow works best. Use a soft treat, a chunk of cheese or a piece of cooked chicken rather than a dry biscuit. By the time the dog has finished chewing a dry treat, he will forget why he is being rewarded in the first place! Incidentally, using food rewards will not teach a dog to beg at the table—the only way to teach a dog to beg at the table is to give him

Once you have bonded with your puppy, he will follow you to the ends of the earth. Be the leader and he will happily be your devoted disciple.

PRACTICE MAKES PERFECT

• Have training lessons with your dog every day in several short segments—three to five times a day for a few minutes at a time is ideal.

• Do not have long practice sessions. The dog will become easily bored.

• Never practice when you are tired, ill, worried or in an otherwise negative mood. This will transmit to the dog and may have an adverse effect on his performance.

Think fun, short and, above all, POSITIVE! End each session on a high note, rather than a failed exercise, and make sure to give a lot of praise. Enjoy the training and help your dog enjoy it, too.

food from the table. In training, rewarding the dog with a food treat will help him associate praise and the treats with learning new behaviors that obviously please his owner.

TRAINING BEGINS: ASK THE DOG A QUESTION

In order to teach your dog anything, you must first get his attention. After all, he cannot learn anything if he is looking away from you with his mind on something else.

To get his attention, ask him "School?" and immediately walk over to him and give him a treat as you tell him "Good dog." Wait a minute or two and repeat the routine, this time with a treat in your hand as you approach within a foot of the dog. Do not go directly to him, but stop about a foot short of him and hold out the treat as you ask "School?" He will see you approaching with a treat in your hand and most likely begin walking toward you. As you meet, give him the treat and praise again.

The third time, ask the question, have a treat in your hand and walk only a short distance toward the dog so that he must walk almost all the way to you. As he reaches you, give him the treat and praise again.

By this time, the dog will probably be getting the idea that if he pays attention to you, espe-

> **COMMAND STANCE**
> Stand up straight and authoritatively when giving your dog commands. Do not issue commands when lying on the floor or lying on your back on the sofa. If you are on your hands and knees when you give a command, your dog will think you are positioning yourself to play.

cially when you ask that question, it will pay off in treats and enjoyable activities for him. In other words, he learns that "school" means doing enjoyable things with you that result in treats and positive attention for him.

Remember that the dog does not understand your verbal language; he only recognizes sounds. Your question translates to a series of sounds for him, and those sounds become the signal to go to you and pay attention; if he does, he will get to interact with you plus receive treats and praise.

THE BASIC COMMANDS

TEACHING SIT

Now that you have the dog's attention, attach his leash and hold it in your left hand and a food treat in your right. Place your food hand at the dog's nose and let him lick the treat but not take it from you. Say "Sit" and slowly raise your food hand from in front of the dog's nose up over his head so that he is looking at the ceiling. As he bends his head upward, he will have to bend his knees to maintain his balance. As he bends his knees, he will assume a sit position. At that point, release the food treat and praise lavishly with comments such as "Good dog! Good sit!," etc. Remember to always praise enthusiastically, because dogs relish verbal praise from their owners and feel so proud of themselves whenever they accomplish a behavior.

You will not use food forever in getting the dog to obey your

Get your Dobe's attention with a treat and lots of praise to prepare him for the lesson ahead.

LANGUAGE BARRIER

Dogs do not understand our language. They can be trained to react to a certain sound, at a certain volume. If you say "No, Oliver" in a very soft, pleasant voice, it will not have the same meaning as "No, Oliver!!" when you raise your voice. You should never use the dog's name during a reprimand, just the command "No." Even though dogs don't understand words, your dog will learn what sounds signify his name. You never want your dog to associate his name with a reprimand.

commands. Food is only used to teach new behaviors, and once the dog knows what you want when you give a specific command, you will wean him off the food treats but still maintain the verbal praise. After all, you will always have your voice with you,

The Doberman Pinscher is sitting obediently by his owner's left side, awaiting his next command. Once the sit command is understood, it becomes the springboard for subsequent lessons.

and there will be many times when you have no food rewards but expect the dog to obey.

Teaching Down

Teaching the down exercise is easy when you understand how the dog perceives the down position, and it is very difficult when you do not. Dogs perceive the down position as a submissive one; therefore, teaching the down exercise using a forceful method can sometimes make the dog develop such a fear of the down that he either runs away when you say "Down" or he attempts to snap at the person who tries to force him down.

Have the dog sit close alongside your left leg, facing in the same direction as you are. Hold the leash in your left hand and a food treat in your right. Now place your left hand lightly on the top of the dog's shoulders where they meet above the spinal cord. Do not push down on the dog's shoulders; simply rest your left hand there so you can guide the dog to lie down close to your left leg rather than to swing away from your side when he drops.

Now place the food hand at the dog's nose, say "Down" very softly (almost a whisper), and slowly lower the food hand to the dog's front feet. When the food hand reaches the floor, begin moving it forward along the floor in front of the dog. Keep talking softly to the dog, saying things like, "Do you want this treat? You can do this, good dog." Your reassuring tone of voice will help calm the dog as he tries to follow the food hand in order to get the treat.

The down-stay command is a natural extension of the down, once the dog has learned the down reliably.

When the dog's elbows touch the floor, release the food and praise softly. Try to get the dog to maintain that down position for several seconds before you let him sit up again. The goal here is to

Establish times for play and times for lessons. All dogs appreciate structure in their lives.

get the dog to settle down and not feel threatened in the down position.

TEACHING STAY

It is easy to teach the dog to stay in either a sit or a down position. Again, we use food and praise during the teaching process as we help the dog to understand exactly what it is that we are expecting him to do.

To teach the sit/stay, start with the dog sitting on your left side as before and hold the leash in your left hand. Have a food treat in your right hand and place your food hand at the dog's nose. Say "Stay" and step out on your right foot to stand directly in front of the dog, toe to toe, as he licks and nibbles the treat. Be sure to keep his head facing upward to maintain the sit position. Count to five and then swing around to stand next to the dog again with him on your left. As soon as you get back to the original position, release the food and praise lavishly.

To teach the down/stay, do the down as previously described. As soon as the dog lies down, say "Stay" and step out on your right foot just as you did in the sit/stay.

An attentive student, eager for his next lesson.

Count to five and then return to stand beside the dog with him on your left side. Release the treat and praise as always.

Within a week or ten days, you can begin to add a bit of distance between you and your dog when you leave him. When you do, use your left hand open with the palm facing the dog as a stay signal, much the same as the hand signal a police officer uses to stop traffic at an intersection. Hold the food treat in your right hand as before, but this time the food is not touching the dog's nose. He will watch the food hand and quickly learn that he is going to get that treat as soon as you return to his side.

When you can stand 3 feet away from your dog for 30 seconds, you can then begin building time and distance in both stays. Eventually, the dog can be expected to remain in the stay position for prolonged periods of time until you return to him or call him to you. Always praise lavishly when he stays.

The stay command is especially useful under many different circumstances, such as "stacking" your Doberman Pinscher at a dog show.

Teaching Come

If you make teaching the come command an enjoyable experience, you should never have a student that does not love the game or that fails to come when called. The secret, it seems, is never to teach the word "come."

At times when an owner most wants his dog to come when called, the owner is likely upset or anxious and he allows these feelings to come through in the tone of his voice when he calls his dog. Hearing that desperation in his owner's voice, the dog fears the results of going to him and therefore either disobeys outright or runs in the opposite direction. The secret, therefore, is to teach the dog a game and, when you want him to come to you, simply

Once your Doberman Pinscher has mastered the basics, practice these exercises with him regularly. Reinforcing training makes for a more reliable performer.

play the game. It is practically a no-fail solution!

To begin, have several members of your family take a few food treats and each go into a different room in the house. Take turns calling the dog, and each person should celebrate the dog's finding him with a treat and lots of happy praise. When a person calls the dog, he is actually inviting the dog to find him and get a treat as a reward for "winning."

A few turns of the "Where are you?" game and the dog will understand that everyone is playing the game and that each person has a big celebration awaiting the dog's success at locating him. Once the dog learns to love the game, simply calling out "Where are you?" will bring him running from wherever he is when he hears that all-important question.

"WHERE ARE YOU?"

When calling the dog, do not say "Come." Say things like, "Rover, where are you? See if you can find me! I have a biscuit for you!" Keep up a constant line of chatter with coaxing sounds and frequent questions such as "Where are you?" The dog will learn to follow the sound of your voice to locate you and receive his reward.

The come command is recognized as one of the most important things to teach a dog, but there are trainers who work with thousands of dogs and never teach the actual word "come." Yet these dogs will race to respond to a person who uses the dog's name followed by "Where are you?" For example, a woman has a 12-year-old companion dog who went blind, but who never fails to locate her owner when asked, "Where are you?"

Children, in particular, love to play this game with their dogs. Children can hide in smaller places like a shower stall or bathtub, behind a bed or under a table. The dog needs to work a little bit harder to find these hiding places, but, when he does, he loves to celebrate with a treat and a tussle with a favorite youngster.

"COME" . . . BACK

Never call your dog to come to you for a correction or scold him when he reaches you. That is the quickest way to turn a come command into "Go away fast!" Dogs think only in the present tense, and your dog will connect the scolding with coming to you, not with the misbehavior of a few moments earlier.

Teaching Heel

Heeling means that the dog walks beside the owner without pulling. It takes time and patience on the owner's part to succeed at teaching the dog that he (the owner) will not proceed unless the dog is walking calmly beside him. Pulling out ahead on the leash is definitely not acceptable.

Begin by holding the leash in your left hand as the dog sits beside your left leg. Move the loop end of the leash to your right hand but keep your left hand short on the leash so it keeps the dog in close next to you.

Say "Heel" and step forward on your left foot. Keep the dog close to you and take three steps. Stop and have the dog sit next to you in what we now call the heel position. Praise verbally, but do not touch the dog. Hesitate a moment and begin again with

Introduce hand signals after your Doberman Pinscher comprehends the vocal commands. Many trainers recommend using hand signals and vocal commands in combination.

Off-leash heeling is an advanced obedience exercise that should be practiced in an enclosed area. The dog starts out sitting in the heel position, awaiting the trainer's signal to begin walking.

"Heel," taking three steps and stopping, at which point the dog is told to sit again.

Your goal here is to have the dog walk those three steps without pulling on the leash. When he will walk calmly beside you for three steps without pulling, increase the number of steps you take to five. When he will walk politely beside you while you take five steps, you can increase the length of your walk to ten steps. Keep increasing the length of your stroll until the dog will walk quietly beside you without pulling as long as you want him to heel. When you stop heeling, indicate to the dog that the exercise is over by verbally praising as you pet him and say "OK, good dog." The "OK" is used as a release word, meaning that the exercise is finished and the dog is free to relax.

If you are dealing with a dog who insists on pulling you around, simply "put on your brakes" and stand your ground until the dog realizes that the two of you are not going anywhere until he is beside you and moving at your pace, not his. It may take some time just standing there to convince the dog that you are the leader and you will be the one to decide on the direction and speed of your travel.

TUG OF WALK

If you begin teaching the heel by taking long walks and letting the dog pull you along, he misinterprets this action as an acceptable form of taking a walk. When you pull back on the leash to counteract his pulling, he reads that tug as a signal to pull even harder!

Each time the dog looks up at you or slows down to give a slack leash between the two of you, quietly praise him and say "Good heel. Good dog." Eventually, the dog will begin to respond and within a few days he will be walking politely beside you without pulling on the leash. At first, the training sessions should be kept short and very positive; soon the dog will be able to walk nicely with you for increasingly longer distances. Remember also to give the dog free time and the opportunity to run and play when you have finished heel practice.

WEANING OFF FOOD IN TRAINING

Food is used in training new behaviors. Once the dog understands what behavior goes with a specific command, it is time to start weaning him off the food treats. At first, give a treat after each exercise. Then, start to give a treat only after every other exercise. Vary the times when you offer a food reward and the times when you only offer praise so that the dog will never know when he is going to receive both food and praise and when he is going to receive only praise. This is called a variable ratio reward system and it proves successful because there is always the chance that the owner will produce a treat, so the dog never stops trying for that reward. No matter what, *always* give verbal praise.

Keep your Doberman motivated but always calm and under your control.

OBEDIENCE CLASSES

It is a good idea to enroll in an obedience class if one is available in your area. If yours is a show dog, handling classes

The heel exercise teaches your Doberman Pinscher to follow at your side, regardless of the speed of your pace. This show dog heels by his handler's side as he is gaited in the ring.

would be even better. Many areas have dog clubs that offer basic obedience training as well as preparatory classes for obedience competition. There are also local dog trainers who offer similar classes.

At obedience trials, dogs can earn titles at various levels of competition. The beginning levels of competition include basic behaviors such as sit, down, heel, etc. The more advanced levels of competition include jumping, retrieving, scent discrimination and signal work. The advanced levels require a dog and owner to put a lot of time and effort into their training, and the titles that can be earned at these levels of competition are very prestigious.

OTHER ACTIVITIES FOR LIFE

Whether a dog is trained in the structured environment of a class or alone with his owner at home, there are many activities that can bring fun and rewards to both owner and dog once they have mastered basic control.

Teaching the dog to help out around the home, in the yard or on the farm provides great satisfaction to both dog and owner. In addition, the dog's help makes life a little easier for his owner and raises his stature as a valued companion to his family. It helps give the dog a purpose by occupying his mind and providing an outlet for his energy.

Backpacking is an exciting and healthful activity that the dog can be taught without assistance

HELPING PAWS

Your dog may not be the next Lassie, but every pet has the potential to do some tricks well. Identify his natural talents and hone them. Is your dog always happy and upbeat? Teach him to wag his tail or give you his paw on command. Real homebodies can be trained to do household chores, such as carrying dirty laundry or retrieving the morning paper.

from more than his owner. The exercise of walking and climbing is good for man and dog alike, and the bond that they develop together is priceless. The rule of thumb is not to allow the dog to carry more than one-sixth of his body weight.

If you are interested in participating in organized competition with your Doberman Pinscher, there are activities other than obedience in which you and your dog can become involved. Agility is a popular and enjoyable sport where dogs run through an obstacle course that includes various jumps, tunnels and other exercises to test the dog's speed and coordination. The owners run through the course beside their dogs to give commands and to guide them through the course. Although competitive, the focus is on fun—it's fun to do, fun to watch and great exercise.

As a Doberman Pinscher owner, you have the opportunity to participate in Schutzhund competition if you choose. Schutzhund originated as a test to determine the best quality dogs to be used for breeding stock. Breeders continue to use it as a way to evaluate working ability and temperament. There are three levels in Schutzhund trials: SchH. I, SchH. II and SchH. III, with each level being progressively more difficult to complete successfully. Each level

NATURAL PRODIGY

Occasionally, a dog and owner who have not attended formal classes have been able to earn entry-level titles by obtaining competition rules and regulations from a local kennel club and practicing on their own to a degree of perfection. Obtaining the higher level titles, however, almost always requires extensive training under the tutelage of experienced instructors. In addition, the more difficult levels require more specialized equipment whereas the lower levels do not.

Afforded the opportunity, the Doberman Pinscher will astound you with his versatility and skill. This sweater-clad Doberman Pinscher enjoys winter sports with his owners, gladly watching the Huskies race through ice and snow.

consists of training, obedience and protection phases. Training for Schutzhund is intense and must be practiced consistently to keep the dog keen. The experience of Schutzhund training is very rewarding for dog and owner, and the Doberman Pinscher's tractability is well suited to this type of training. To find out more about Schutzhund, contact a local breed club or training club.

The weave poles are a part of agility trials. Doberman Pinschers are extremely intelligent and trainable dogs who thrive on performing and pleasing their owners.

The Doberman is a natural frisbee dog and revels in a game of fetch with his master.

Physical Structure of the Doberman Pinscher

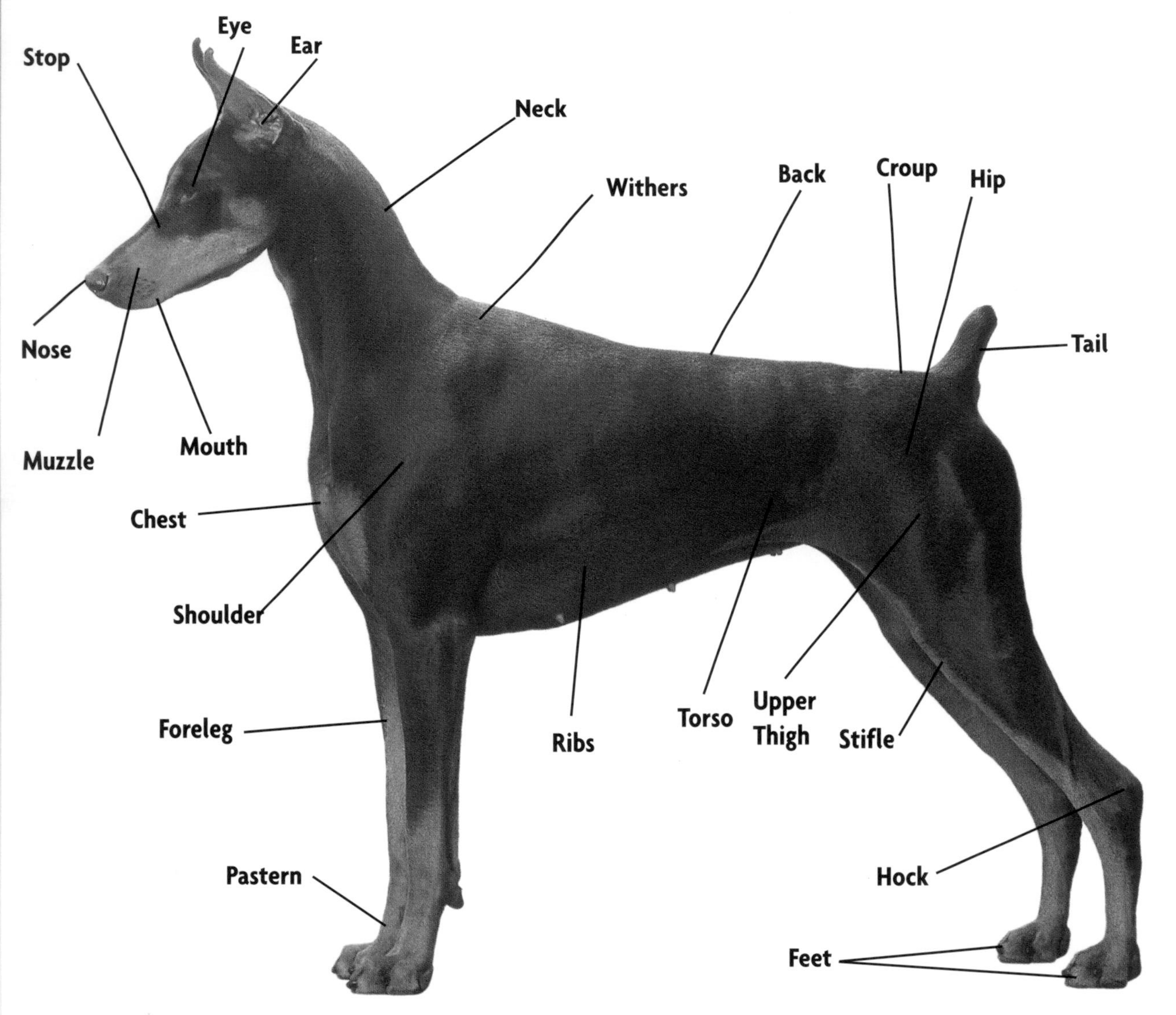

HEALTH CARE OF YOUR
DOBERMAN PINSCHER

Dogs suffer from many of the same physical illnesses as people. They might even share many of the same psychological problems. Since people usually know more about human diseases than canine maladies, many of the terms used in this chapter will be familiar but not necessarily those used by veterinarians. For example, we will use the term *x-ray*, instead of the more acceptable term *radiograph*. We will also use the familiar term *symptoms* even though dogs don't have symptoms, which are verbal descriptions of the patient's feelings; dogs have *clinical signs*. Since dogs can't speak, we have to look for clinical signs...but we still use the term *symptoms* in this book.

As a general rule, medicine is *practiced*. That term is not arbitrary. Medicine is a constantly changing art as we learn more and more about genetics, electronic aids (like CAT scans and MRIs) and daily laboratory advances. There are many dog maladies, like canine hip dysplasia, which are not universally treated in the same manner. For example, some veterinarians opt for surgery more often than others do.

SELECTING A QUALIFIED VET

Your selection of a veterinarian should be based not only upon his personality and abilities with large-breed dogs but also upon his convenience to your home. You want a vet who is close because you might have emergencies or need to make multiple visits for treatments. You want a vet who has services that you might require such as tattooing and possibly grooming or boarding facilities, as well as a good reputation for ability and responsiveness. There is nothing more frustrating than having to wait to get a response from your veterinarian.

All veterinarians should be licensed and capable of dealing with routine health issues like

Before you buy a dog, meet and talk to the vets in your area. Take everything into consideration; discuss background, specialties, fees, emergency policies, etc.

Internal Organs of the Doberman Pinscher

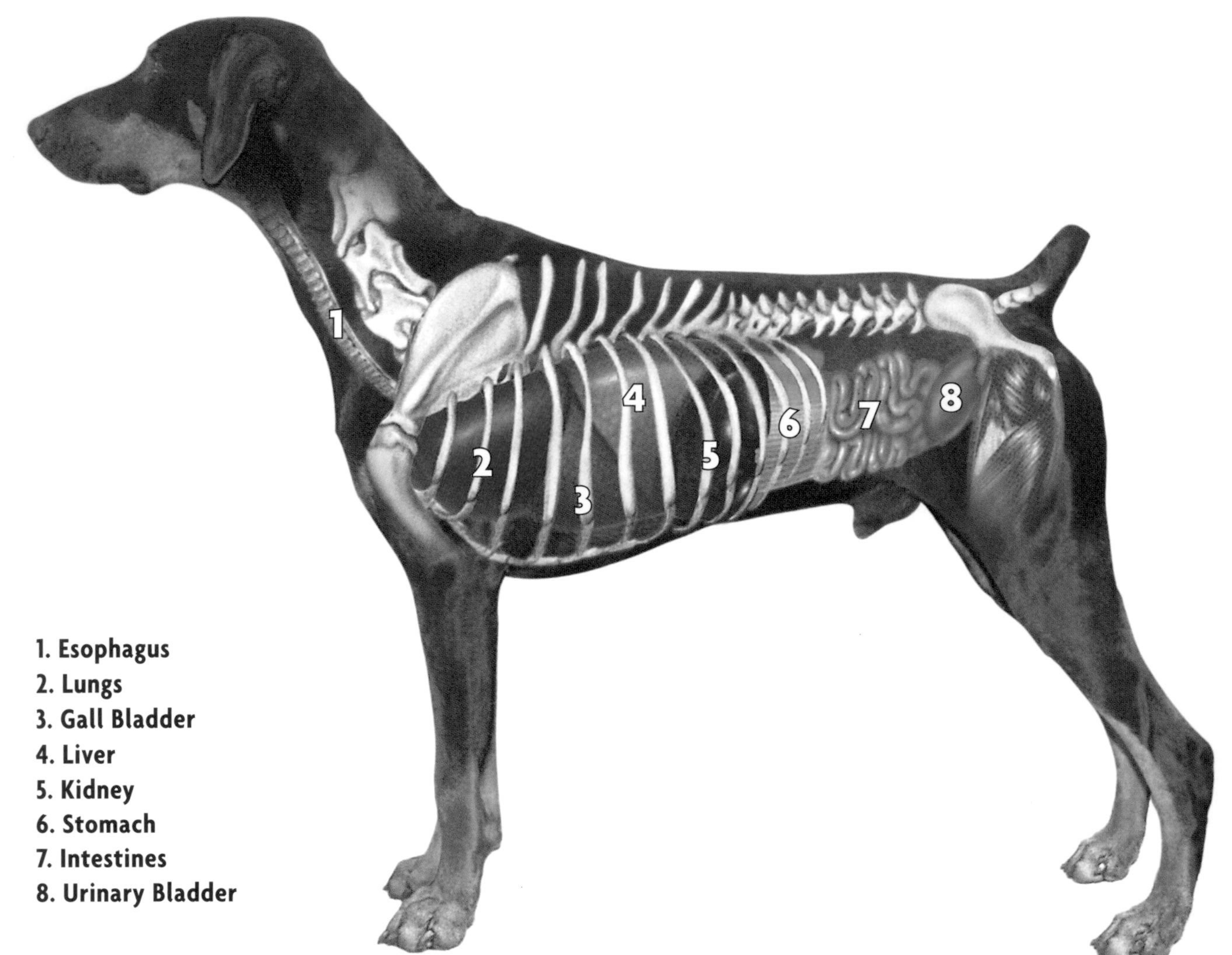

check-ups, injuries, vaccinations, etc. Most veterinarians do routine surgery such as neutering, stitching up wounds, docking tails and cropping ears. There are, however, many veterinary specialties that require further studies and internships. There are specialists in heart problems (veterinary cardiologists), skin problems (veterinary dermatologists), teeth and gum problems (veterinary dentists), eye problems (veterinary ophthalmologists) and x-rays (veterinary radiologists), and vets who have specialties in bones, muscles or certain organs. When the problem affecting your dog is serious, it is not unusual or impudent to get another medical opinion, although it is courteous to advise the vets concerned about this. You might also want to compare costs among several veterinarians. Sophisticated health care and veterinary services can be very costly. Don't be bashful about discussing these costs with your veterinarian.

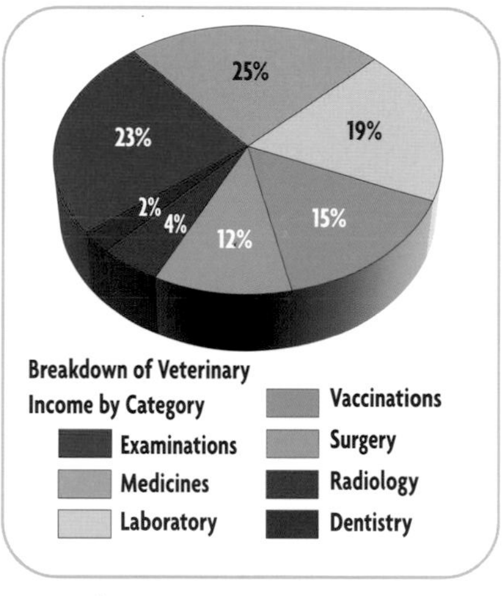

A typical vet's income, categorized according to services provided. This survey dealt with small-animal practices.

PREVENTATIVE MEDICINE

It is much easier, less costly and more effective to practice preventative medicine than to fight bouts of illness and disease. Properly bred puppies come from parents that were selected based upon their genetic-disease profiles. Their mother should have been vaccinated, free of all internal and external parasites and properly nourished. For these reasons, a visit to the veterinarian who cared for the dam is recommended. While the dam can pass on disease resistance to her puppies, which can last for eight to ten weeks, she can also pass on parasites and many infections. It is always advisable to learn as much about the dam's health as possible.

NEUTERING/SPAYING

Male dogs are castrated. The operation removes both testicles and requires that the dog be anesthetized. Recovery takes about one week. Females are spayed; in this operation, the uterus (womb) and both of the ovaries are removed. This is major surgery, also carried out under general anesthesia, and it usually takes a bitch two weeks to recover.

Skeletal Structure of the Doberman Pinscher

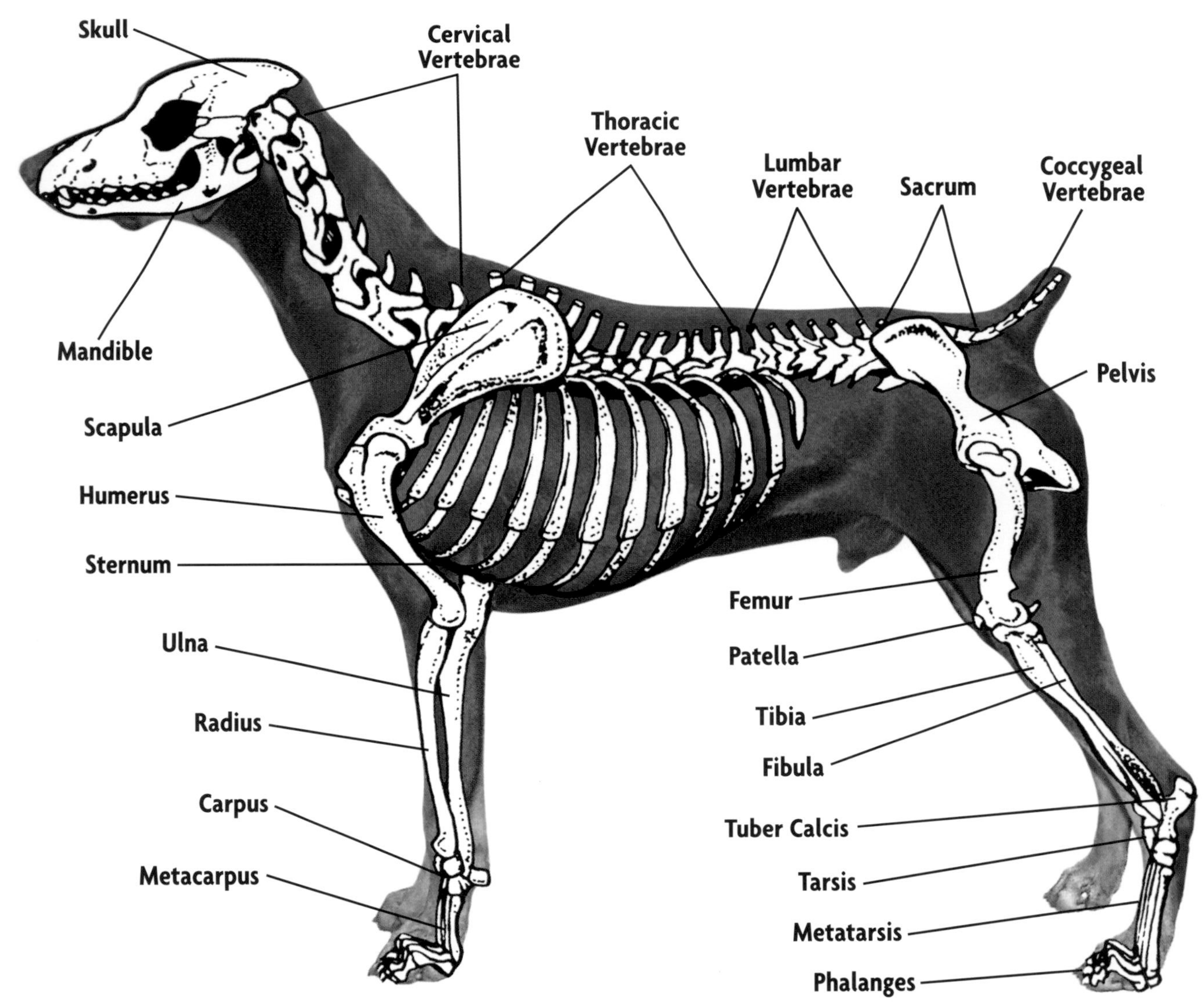

Weaning to Five Months Old

Puppies should be weaned by the time they are about two months old. A puppy that remains for at least eight weeks with his mother and littermates usually adapts better to other dogs and people later in his life.

You should have your newly acquired puppy examined by a veterinarian immediately, either on your way home from the breeder's or as soon as possible after. The puppy will have his teeth examined and have his skeletal conformation and general health checked prior to certification by the veterinarian. Many puppies have problems with their kneecaps, cataracts and other eye problems, heart murmurs and undescended testicles.

DENTAL CARE FOR DOGS

A dental examination is in order when the dog is between six months and one year of age so any permanent teeth that have erupted incorrectly can

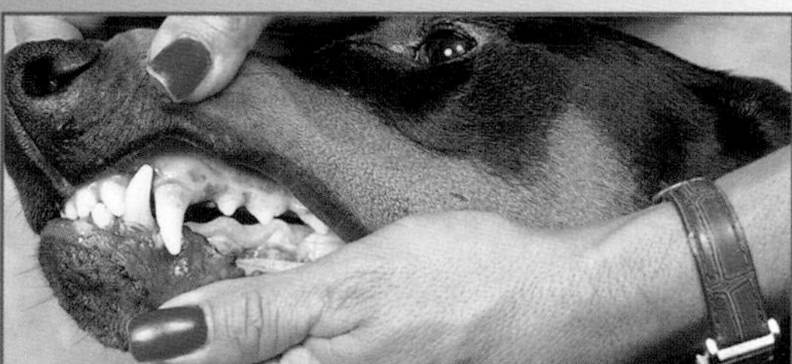

be corrected. It is important to begin a brushing routine at home, using dental-care products made for dogs, such as canine toothbrushes and specially formulated toothpaste. Durable nylon and safe edible chews should be a part of your puppy's arsenal for good health, good teeth and pleasant breath. The vast majority of dogs three to four years old and older have diseases of the gums from lack of dental attention. Using the various types of dental chews can be very effective in controlling dental plaque.

PARVO FOR THE COURSE

Canine parvovirus is a highly contagious disease that attacks puppies and older dogs. Spread through contact with infected feces, parvovirus causes bloody diarrhea, vomiting, heart damage, dehydration, shock and death. To prevent this tragedy, have your puppy begin his series of vaccinations at six to eight weeks of age. Be aware that the virus is easily spread and is carried on a dog's hair, feet, water bowls and other objects, as well as on people's shoes and clothing.

Vaccination Scheduling

Most vaccinations are given by injection and should only be done by a veterinarian. Both he and you should keep a record of the date of the injection, the identification of the vaccine and the amount given. Some vets give a first vaccination at six weeks, but most dog breeders prefer the course not to commence until about eight weeks because of the risk of negating any antibodies passed on by the dam. The vaccination

Normal hairs of a dog enlarged 200 times original size. The cuticle (outer covering) is clean and healthy. Unlike human hair that grows from the base, a dog's hair also grows from the end, as shown in the inset.

SEM by Dr Dennis Kunkel, University of Hawaii

scheduling is usually based on a 15-day cycle. You must take your vet's advice as to when to vaccinate, as this may differ according to the vaccine used. Most vaccinations immunize your puppy against viruses. The usual vaccines contain immunizing doses of several different viruses such as distemper, parvovirus, parainfluenza and hepatitis. There are other vaccines available when the puppy is at risk. You should rely upon professional advice. This is especially true for the booster-shot program. Most vaccination programs require a booster when the puppy is a year old and once a year thereafter. In some cases, circumstances may require more or less frequent immunizations.

Kennel cough, more formally known as tracheobronchitis, is treated with a vaccine that is sprayed into the dog's nostrils. Kennel cough is usually included in routine vaccination, but this is often not so effective as for other major diseases.

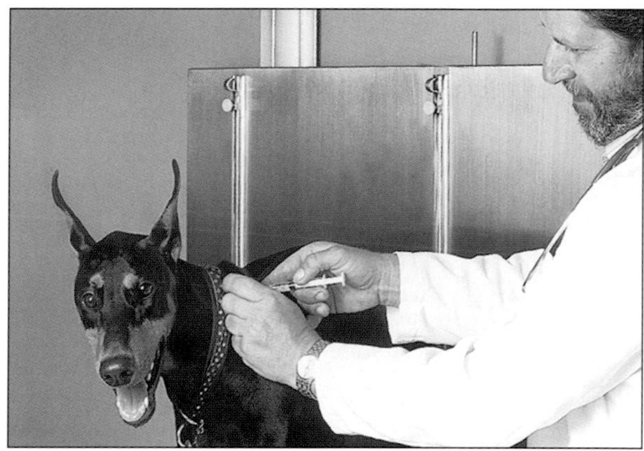

Your adult Dobe must be taken to the vet annually, with certain vaccinations followed up every one to three years.

PUPPY VACCINATIONS

Your veterinarian will probably recommend that your puppy be fully vaccinated before you take him outside. There are airborne diseases, parasite eggs in the grass and unexpected visits from other dogs that might be dangerous to your puppy's health. Other dogs are the most harmful reservoir of pathogenic organisms, as everything they have can be transmitted to your puppy.

Five Months to One Year of Age

Unless you intend to breed or show your dog, neutering the puppy at six months of age is recommended. Discuss this with your veterinarian; most professionals advise neutering the puppy, but opinions differ on the best age at which to have this done. Neutering/spaying has proven to be extremely beneficial to both male and female dogs, respectively. Besides eliminating the possibility of pregnancy, it inhibits (but does not prevent) breast cancer in bitches and prostate cancer in male dogs.

Your veterinarian should provide your puppy with a thorough dental evaluation at six months of age, ascertaining whether all the permanent teeth have erupted properly. A home dental-care regimen should be

HEALTH AND VACCINATION SCHEDULE

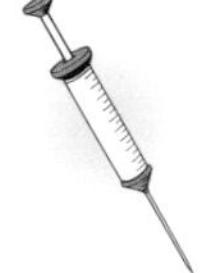

AGE IN WEEKS:	6TH	8TH	10TH	12TH	14TH	16TH	20-24TH	52ND
Worm Control	✔	✔	✔	✔	✔	✔	✔	
Neutering								✔
Heartworm		✔		✔		✔	✔	
Parvovirus	✔		✔		✔		✔	✔
Distemper		✔		✔		✔		✔
Hepatitis		✔		✔		✔		✔
Leptospirosis								✔
Parainfluenza	✔		✔		✔			✔
Dental Examination		✔					✔	✔
Complete Physical		✔					✔	✔
Coronavirus				✔			✔	✔
Kennel Cough	✔							
Hip Dysplasia								✔
Rabies							✔	

Vaccinations are not instantly effective. It takes about two weeks for the dog's immune system to develop antibodies. Most vaccinations require annual booster shots. Your veterinarian should guide you in this regard.

initiated at six months, including brushing weekly and providing good dental devices (such as nylon bones). Regular dental care promotes healthy teeth, fresh breath and a longer life.

OVER ONE YEAR OF AGE

Once a year, your grown dog should visit the vet for an examination and vaccination boosters. Some vets recommend blood tests, thyroid level check and dental evaluation to accompany these annual visits. A thorough clinical evaluation by the vet can provide critical background information for your dog. Blood tests are often performed at one year of age, and dental examinations will accompany your dog's check-ups. In the long run, quality preventative care for your pet can save money, teeth and lives.

SKIN PROBLEMS IN DOBERMAN PINSCHERS

Veterinarians are consulted by dog owners for skin problems more than for any other group of diseases or maladies. Dogs' skin can be as sensitive as human skin and both can suffer from almost the same ailments, including acne, which occurs on the chins of Doberman Pinschers. For this reason, veterinary dermatology has developed into a specialty practiced by many veterinarians.

Since many skin problems have visual symptoms that are almost identical, it requires the skill of an experienced veterinary dermatologist to identify and cure many of the more severe skin disorders. Pet shops sell many treatments for skin problems but most of the treatments are directed at symptoms and not the underlying problem(s). If your dog is suffering from a skin disorder, you should seek professional assistance as quickly as possible. As with all diseases, the earlier a problem is identified and treated, the more successful is the cure.

Hereditary Skin Disorders

Veterinary dermatologists are currently researching a number of skin disorders that are believed to have a hereditary basis. These inherited diseases are transmitted by both parents, who appear (phenotypically) normal but have a recessive gene for the disease, meaning that they carry, but are not affected by, the disease. These disease pose serious problems to

DISEASE REFERENCE CHART

	What is it?	What causes it?	Symptoms
Leptospirosis	Severe disease that affects the internal organs; can be spread to people.	A bacterium, which is often carried by rodents, that enters through mucous membranes and spreads quickly throughout the body.	Range from fever, vomiting and loss of appetite in less severe cases to shock, irreversible kidney damage and possibly death in most severe cases.
Rabies	Potentially deadly virus that infects warm-blooded mammals.	Bite from a carrier of the virus, mainly wild animals.	1st stage: dog exhibits change in behavior, fear. 2nd stage: dog's behavior becomes more aggressive. 3rd stage: loss of coordination, trouble with bodily functions.
Parvovirus	Highly contagious virus, potentially deadly.	Ingestion of the virus, which is usually spread through the feces of infected dogs.	Most common: severe diarrhea. Also vomiting, fatigue, lack of appetite.
Kennel cough	Contagious respiratory infection.	Combination of types of bacteria and virus. Most common: *Bordetella bronchiseptica* bacteria and parainfluenza virus.	Chronic cough.
Distemper	Disease primarily affecting respiratory and nervous system.	Virus that is related to the human measles virus.	Mild symptoms such as fever, lack of appetite and mucus secretion progress to evidence of brain damage, "hard pad."
Hepatitis	Virus primarily affecting the liver.	Canine adenovirus type I (CAV-1). Enters system when dog breathes in particles.	Lesser symptoms include listlessness, diarrhea, vomiting. More severe symptoms include "blue-eye" (clumps of virus in eye).
Coronavirus	Virus resulting in digestive problems.	Virus is spread through infected dog's feces.	Stomach upset evidenced by lack of appetite, vomiting, diarrhea.

breeders because in some instances there is no method of identifying carriers. Often the secondary diseases associated with these skin conditions are even more debilitating than the skin disorder, including cancers and respiratory problems.

Among the hereditary skin disorders for which the mode of inheritance is known are acrodermatitis, cutaneous asthenia (Ehlers-Danlos syndrome), sebaceous adenitis, cyclic hematopoiesis, dermatomyositis, IgA deficiency, color dilution alopecia and nodular dermatofibrosis. Two of these are known in the Doberman Pinscher: color dilution alopecia, affecting blue Doberman Pinschers, and sebaceous adenitis. Some of these disorders are limited to one or two breeds and others affect a large number of breeds.

Parasite Bites

Many of us are allergic to mosquito bites. The bites itch, erupt and may even become infected. Dogs have the same reaction to fleas, ticks and/or mites. When you feel the prick of the mosquito as it bites you, you have a chance to kill it with your hand. Unfortunately, when your dog is bitten by a flea, tick or mite, he can only scratch it away or bite it. By the time the dog has been bitten, the parasite has done some of its damage. It may also have laid eggs, which will cause further problems in the near future. The itching from parasite bites is probably due to the saliva injected into the site when the parasite sucks the dog's blood.

Auto-Immune Skin Conditions

Auto-immune skin conditions are commonly referred to as being allergic to yourself, while allergies are usually inflammatory reactions to an outside stimulus. Auto-immune diseases cause serious damage to the tissues that are involved.

The best known auto-immune disease is lupus, which affects people as well as dogs. The symptoms are variable and may affect the kidneys, bones, blood chemistry and skin. It can be fatal to both dogs and humans, though it is not thought to be transmissible. It is usually successfully treated with cortisone, prednisone or a similar corticosteroid, but extensive use of these drugs can have harmful side effects.

Airborne Allergies

Just as humans have hay fever, rose fever and other fevers from which they suffer during the pollinating season, many dogs suffer from the same allergies. When the pollen count is high, your dog might suffer but don't expect him to sneeze and have a runny nose as a human would.

First Aid at a Glance

Burns
Place the affected area under cool water; use ice if only a small area is burnt.

Bee stings/Insect bites
Apply ice to relieve swelling; antihistamine dosed properly.

Animal bites
Clean any bleeding area; apply pressure until bleeding subsides; go to the vet.

Spider bites
Use cold compress and a pressurized pack to inhibit venom's spreading.

Antifreeze poisoning
Immediately induce vomiting by using hydrogen peroxide. Seek *immediate* veterinary care.

Fish hooks
Removal best handled by vet; hook must be cut in order to remove.

Snake bites
Pack ice around bite; contact vet quickly; identify snake for proper antivenin.

Car accident
Move dog from roadway with blanket; seek veterinary aid.

Shock
Calm the dog, keep him warm; seek immediate veterinary help.

Nosebleed
Apply cold compress to the nose; apply pressure to any visible abrasion.

Bleeding
Apply pressure above the area; treat wound by applying a cotton pack.

Heat stroke
Submerge dog in cold bath; cool down with fresh air and water; go to the vet.

Frostbite/Hypothermia
Warm the dog with a warm bath, electric blankets or hot water bottles.

Abrasions
Clean the wound and wash out thoroughly with fresh water; apply antiseptic.

Remember: an injured dog may attempt to bite a helping hand from fear and confusion. Always muzzle the dog before trying to offer assistance.

Dogs react to pollen allergies in the same way they react to fleas—they scratch and bite themselves. Doberman Pinschers are very susceptible to airborne pollen allergies. Dogs, like humans, can be tested for allergens. Discuss the testing with your veterinary dermatologist.

CARETAKER OF TEETH

You are your dog's caretaker and his dentist. Vets warn that plaque and tartar buildup on the teeth will damage the gums and allow

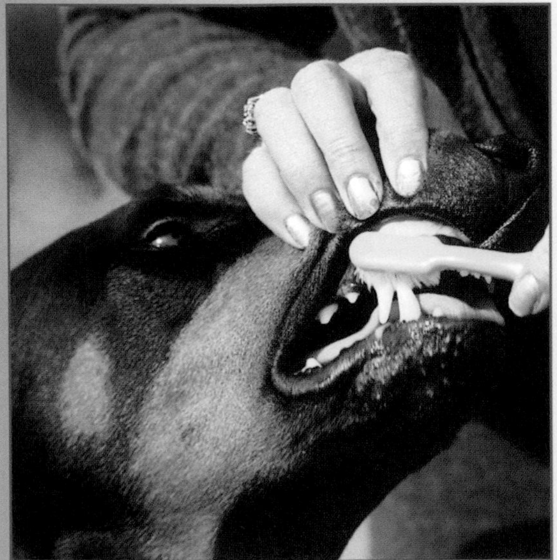

bacteria to enter the dog's bloodstream, causing serious damage to the animal's vital organs. Studies show that over 50 percent of dogs have some form of gum disease before age three. Daily or weekly tooth cleaning (with a brush or soft gauze pad wipes) can add to your dog's life.

FOOD PROBLEMS

Food Allergies

Dogs are allergic to many foods that are best-sellers and highly recommended by breeders and veterinarians. Changing the brand of food that you buy may not eliminate the problem if the element to which the dog is allergic is contained in the new brand.

Recognizing a food allergy is difficult. Humans vomit or have rashes when they eat a food to which they are allergic. Dogs neither vomit nor (usually) develop rashes. They react in the same manner as they do to an airborne or flea allergy; they itch, scratch and bite, thus making the diagnosis extremely difficult. While pollen allergies and parasite bites are usually seasonal, food allergies are year-round problems.

Food Intolerance

Food intolerance is the inability of the dog to completely digest certain foods. For example, puppies that may have done very well on their mother's milk may not do well on cow's milk. The result of this food intolerance may be loose bowels, passing gas and stomach pains. These are the only obvious symptoms of food intolerance and that makes diagnosis difficult.

Treating Food Problems

It is possible to handle food allergies and food intolerance yourself. Put your dog on a diet that he has never had. Obviously, if he has never eaten this new food, he can't yet have been allergic or intolerant of it. Start with a single ingredient that is not in the dog's diet at the present time. Ingredients like chopped beef or chicken are common in dogs' diets, so try something more exotic like rabbit, pheasant or another good source of protein. Keep the dog on this diet (with no additives) for a month. If the symptoms of food allergy or intolerance disappear, chances are your dog has a food allergy.

Don't think that the single ingredient cured the problem. You still must find a suitable diet and ascertain which ingredient in the old diet was objectionable. This is most easily done by adding ingredients to the new diet one at a time. Let the dog stay on the modified diet for a month before you add another ingredient. Eventually, you will determine the ingredient that caused the adverse reaction.

PROPER DIET

Feeding your dog properly is very important. An incorrect diet could affect the dog's health, behavior and nervous system, possibly making a normal dog into an aggressive one. Its most visible effects are to the skin and coat, but internal organs are similarly affected.

Dogs of any age, like humans, can be allergic to pollen and grasses. This is not as uncommon as you might expect.

An alternative method is to study carefully the ingredients in the diet to which your dog is allergic or intolerant. Identify the main ingredient in this diet and eliminate the main ingredient by buying a different food that does not have that ingredient. Keep experimenting until the symptoms disappear after one month on the new diet.

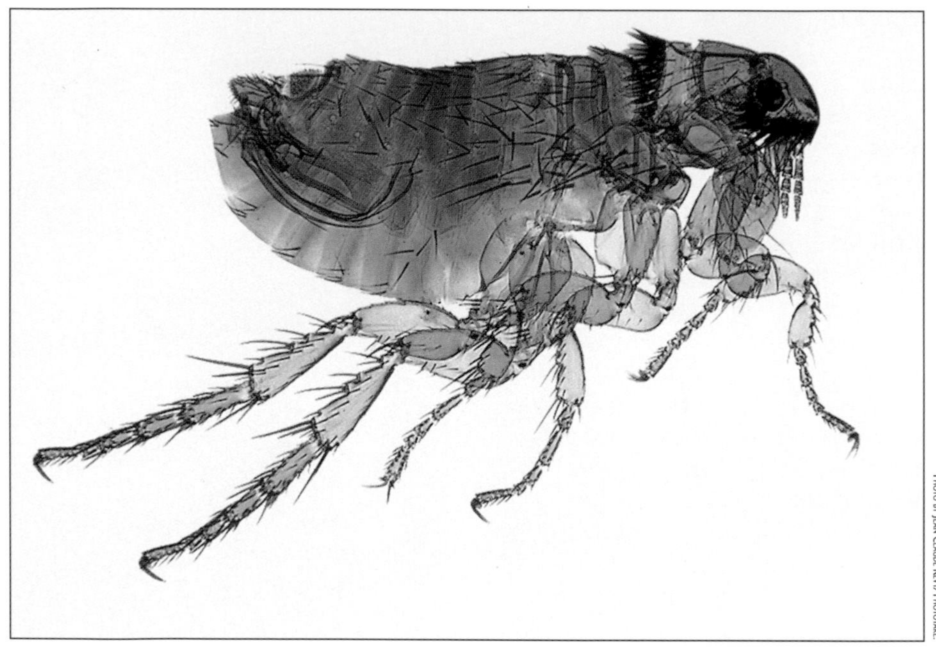

A male dog flea, *Ctenocephalides canis.*

Photo by Jean Claude Revy/Phototake.

EXTERNAL PARASITES

Fleas

Of all the problems to which dogs are prone, none is more well known and frustrating than fleas. Flea infestation is relatively simple to cure but difficult to prevent. Parasites that are harbored inside the body are a bit more difficult to eradicate but they are easier to control.

To control flea infestation, you have to understand the flea's life cycle. Fleas are often thought of as a summertime problem, but centrally heated homes have changed the patterns and fleas can be found at any time of the year. The most effective method of flea control is a two-stage approach: one stage to kill the adult fleas, and the other to control the development of pre-adult fleas. Unfortunately, no single active ingredient is effective against all stages of the life cycle.

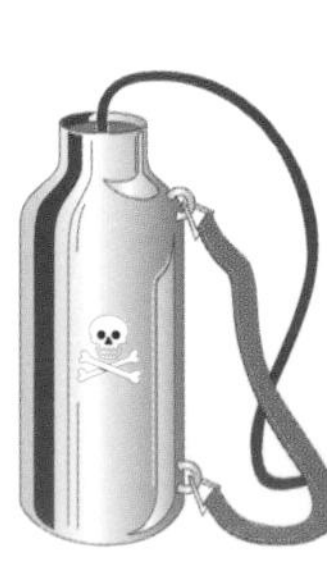

FLEA KILLER CAUTION—"POISON"

Flea-killers are poisonous. You should not spray these toxic chemicals on areas of a dog's body that he licks, including his genitals and his face. Flea killers taken internally are a better answer, but check with your vet in case internal therapy is not advised for your dog.

Life Cycle Stages

During its life, a flea will pass through four life stages: egg, larva, pupa or nymph and adult. The adult stage is the most visible and irritating stage of the flea life cycle, and this is why the majority of flea-control products concentrate on this stage. The fact is that adult fleas account for only 1% of the total flea population, and the other 99% exist in pre-adult stages, i.e., eggs, larvae and nymphs. The pre-adult stages are barely visible to the naked eye.

The Life Cycle of the Flea

Eggs are laid on the dog, usually in quantities of about 20 or 30, several times a day. The adult female flea must have a blood meal before each egg-laying session. When first laid, the eggs will cling to the dog's hair, as the eggs are still moist. However, they will quickly dry out and fall from the dog, especially if the dog moves around or scratches. Many eggs will fall off in the dog's favorite area or an area in which he spends a lot of time, such as his bed.

Once the eggs fall from the dog onto the carpet or furniture, they will hatch into larvae. This takes from one to ten days. Larvae are not particularly mobile and will usually travel only a few inches from where they hatch. However, they do have a tendency to move away from bright light and heavy traffic—under furniture and behind doors are common places to find high quantities of flea larvae.

The flea larvae feed on dead organic matter, including adult flea feces, until they are ready to change into adult fleas. Fleas will usually remain as larvae for around seven days. After this period, the larvae will pupate into protective pupae. While inside the pupae, the larvae will undergo

EN GARDE:
CATCHING FLEAS OFF GUARD!

Consider the following ways to arm yourself against fleas:

- Add a small amount of pennyroyal or eucalyptus oil to your dog's bath. These natural remedies repel fleas.
- Supplement your dog's food with fresh garlic (minced or grated) and a hearty amount of brewer's yeast, both of which ward off fleas.
- Use a flea comb on your dog daily. Submerge fleas in a cup of bleach to kill them quickly.
- Confine the dog to only a few rooms to limit the spread of fleas in the home.
- Vacuum daily...and get all of the crevices! Dispose of the bag every few days until the problem is under control.
- Wash your dog's bedding daily. Cover cushions where your dog sleeps with towels, and wash the towels often.

Fleas have been measured as being able to jump 300,000 times and can jump 150 times their length in any direction, including straight up.

metamorphosis and change into adult fleas. This can take as little time as a few days, but the adult fleas can remain inside the pupae waiting to hatch for up to two years. The pupae are signaled to hatch by certain stimuli, such as physical pressure—the pupae's being stepped on, heat from an animal's lying on the pupae or increased carbon-dioxide levels and vibrations—indicating that a suitable host is available.

Once hatched, the adult flea must feed within a few days. Once the adult flea finds a host, it will not leave voluntarily. It only becomes dislodged by grooming or the host animal's scratching.

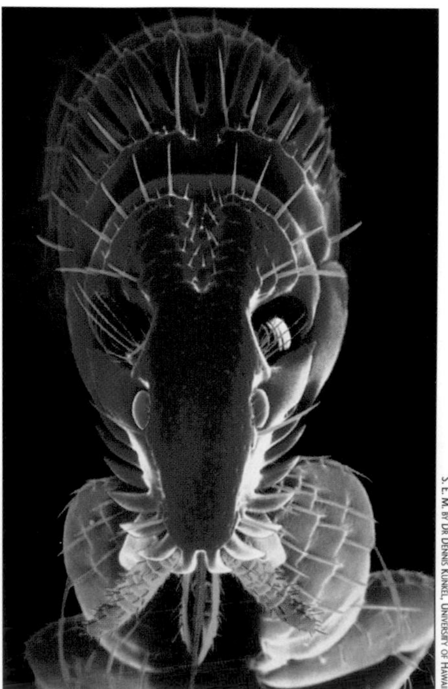

A scanning electron micrograph of a dog or cat flea, *Ctenocephalides*, magnified more than 100x. This image has been colorized for effect.

S.E.M. by Dr. Dennis Kunkel, University of Hawaii.

Photo by Dwight R. Kuhn.

The adult flea will remain on the host for the duration of its life unless forcibly removed.

Treating the Environment and the Dog

Treating fleas should be a two-pronged attack. First, the environment needs to be treated; this includes carpets and furniture, especially the dog's bedding and areas underneath furniture. The environment should be treated with a household spray containing an Insect Growth Regulator (IGR) and an insecticide to kill the adult fleas. Most IGRs are effective against eggs and larvae; they actually mimic the fleas' own hormones and stop the eggs and larvae from developing into adult fleas. There are currently no treatments available to attack the pupa stage of the life cycle, so the adult insecticide is used to kill the newly hatched adult fleas before they find a host. Most IGRs are active for many months, while

THE LIFE CYCLE OF THE FLEA

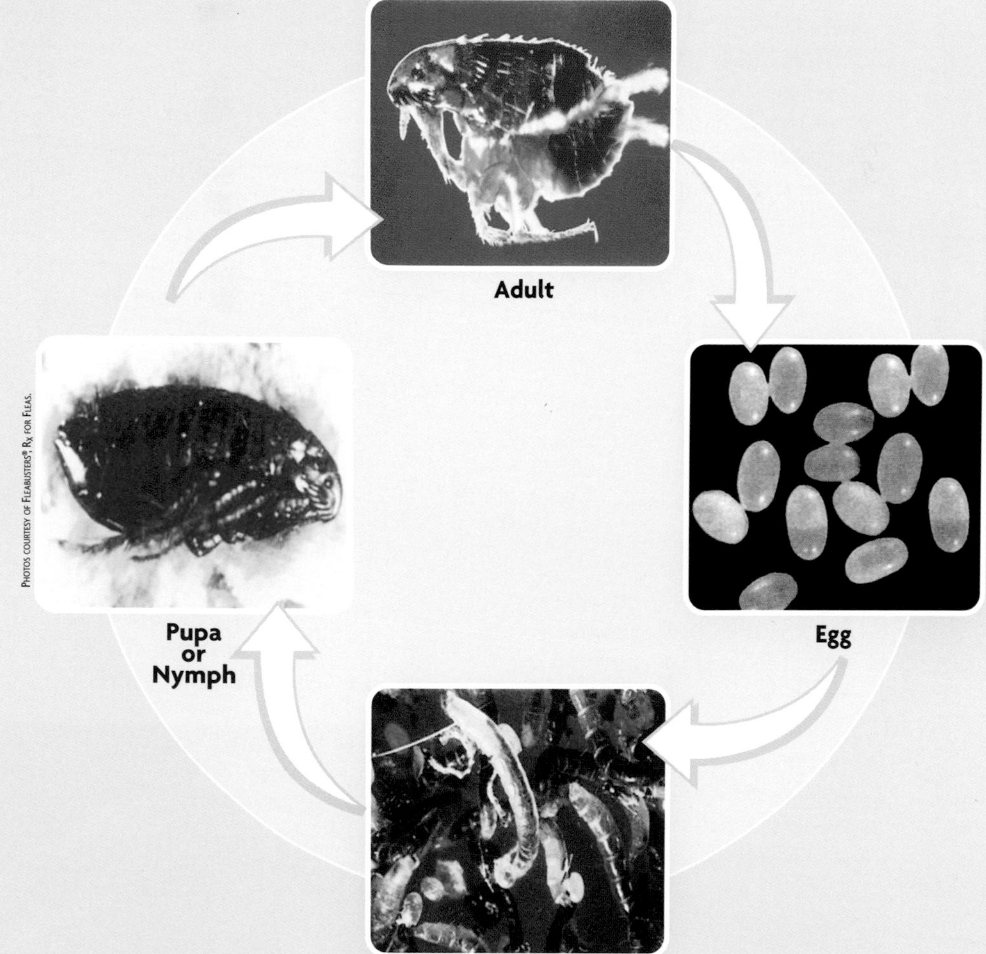

A LOOK AT FLEAS

Fleas have been around for millions of years and have adapted to changing host animals. They are able to go through a complete life cycle in less than one month or they can extend their lives to almost two years by remaining as pupae or cocoons. They do not need blood or any other food for up to 20 months.

INSECT GROWTH REGULATOR (IGR)

Two types of products should be used when treating fleas—a product to treat the pet and a product to treat the home. Adult fleas represent less than 1% of the flea population. The pre-adult fleas (eggs, larvae and pupae) represent more than 99% of the flea population and are found in the environment; it is in the case of pre-adult fleas that products containing an Insect Growth Regulator (IGR) should be used in the home.

IGRs are a new class of compounds used to prevent the development of insects. They do not kill the insect outright, but instead use the insect's biology against it to stop it from completing its growth. Products that contain methoprene are the world's first and leading IGRs. Used to control fleas and other insects, this type of IGR will stop flea larvae from developing and protect the house for up to seven months.

adult insecticides are only active for a few days.

When treating with a household spray, it is a good idea to vacuum before applying the product. This stimulates as many pupae as possible to hatch into adult fleas. The vacuum cleaner should also be treated with an insecticide to prevent the eggs and larvae that have been collected in the vacuum bag from hatching.

The second stage of treatment is to apply an adult insecticide to the dog. Traditionally, this would be in the form of a collar or a spray, but more recent innovations include digestible insecticides that poison the fleas when they ingest the dog's blood. Alternatively, there are drops that, when placed on the back of the dog's neck, spread throughout the dog's hair and skin to kill adult fleas.

TICKS

Though not as common as fleas, ticks are found all over the tropical and temperate world. They don't bite, like fleas; they harpoon. They dig their sharp proboscis (nose) into the dog's skin and drink the blood. Their

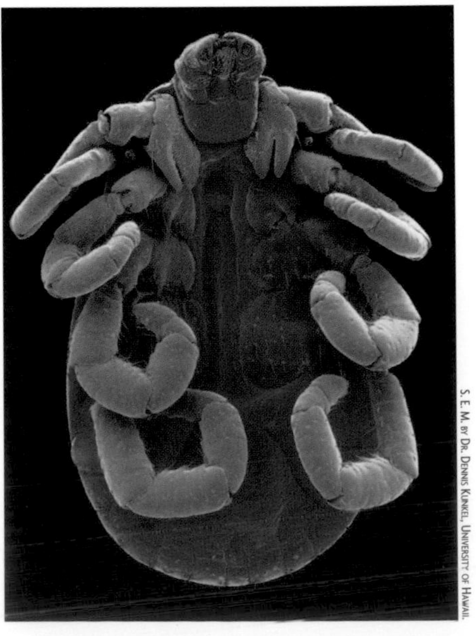

S.E.M. by Dr. Dennis Kunkel, University of Hawaii

The American dog tick, *Dermacentor variabilis*, is probably the most common tick found on dogs. Look at the strength in its eight legs! No wonder it's hard to detach them.

only food and drink is dog's blood. Dogs can get Lyme disease, Rocky Mountain spotted fever, tick bite paralysis and many other diseases from ticks. They may live where fleas are found and they like to hide in cracks or seams in walls. They are controlled the same way fleas are controlled.

The American dog tick, *Dermacentor variabilis*, may well be the most common dog tick in many geographical areas, especially those areas where the climate is hot and humid. Most dog ticks have life expectancies of a week to six months, depending upon climatic conditions. They can neither jump nor fly, but they can crawl slowly and can range up to 16 feet to reach a sleeping or unsuspecting dog.

DEER-TICK CROSSING

The great outdoors may be fun for your dog, but it also is a home to dangerous ticks. Deer ticks carry a bacterium known as *Borrelia burgdorferi* and are most active in the autumn and spring. When infections are caught early, penicillin and tetracycline are effective antibiotics, but, if left untreated, the bacteria may cause neurological, kidney and cardiac problems as well as long-term trouble with walking and painful joints.

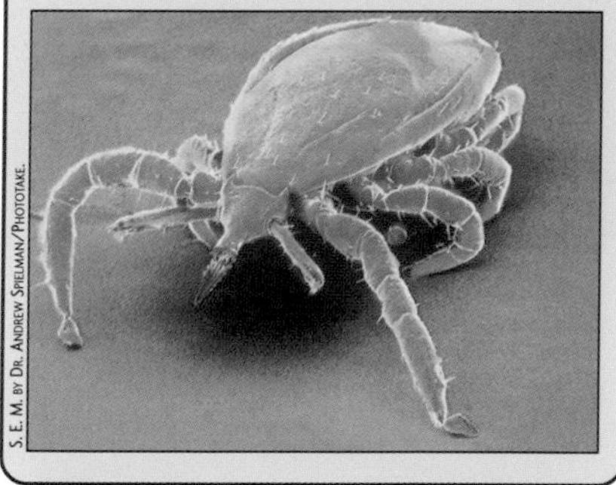

S. E. M. by Dr. Andrew Spielman/Phototake.

MITES

Just as fleas and ticks can be problematic for your dog, mites can also lead to an itchy nuisance. Microscopic in size, mites are related to ticks and generally take up permanent residence on their host animal—in this case, your dog! The term *mange* refers to any infestation caused by one of the mighty mites, of which there are six varieties that concern dog owners.

Demodex mites cause a condition known as demodicosis

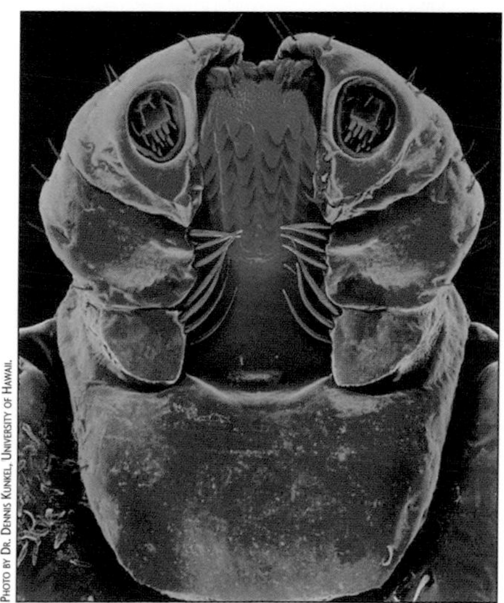

Photo by Dr. Dennis Kunkel, University of Hawaii.

The head of an American dog tick, *Dermacentor variabilis*, enlarged and colorized for effect.

The mange mite, *Psoroptes bovis*, can infest cattle and other domestic animals.

Photo by James Hayden/Yoav/Phototake.

(sometimes called red mange or follicular mange), in which the mites live in the dog's hair follicles and sebaceous glands in larger-than-normal numbers. This type of mange is commonly passed from the dam to her puppies and usually shows up on the puppies' muzzles, though demodicosis is not transferable from one normal dog to another. Most dogs recover from this type of mange without any treatment, though topical therapies are commonly prescribed by the vet.

Human lice look like dog lice; the two are closely related.

Photo by Dwight R. Kuhn.

The *Cheyletiellosis* mite is the hook-mouthed culprit associated with "walking dandruff," a condition that affects dogs as well as cats and rabbits. This mite lives on the surface of the animal's skin and is readily transferable through direct or indirect contact with an affected animal. The dandruff is present in the form of scaly skin, which may or may not be itchy. If not treated, this mange can affect a whole kennel of dogs and can be spread to humans as well.

The *Sarcoptes* mite causes intense itching on the dog in the form of a condition known as scabies or sarcoptic mange. The cycle of the *Sarcoptes* mite lasts about three weeks, and the mites live in the top layer of the dog's skin (epidermis), preferably in areas with little hair. Scabies is highly contagious and can be passed to humans. Sometimes an allergic reaction to the mite worsens the severe itching associated with sarcoptic mange.

Ear mites, *Otodectes cynotis,* lead to otodectic mange, which most commonly affects the outer ear canal of the dog, though other areas can be affected as well. Dogs with ear-mite infestation commonly scratch at their ears, causing further irritation, and shake their heads. Dark brown droppings in the outer ear confirm the diagnosis. Your vet can prescribe a treatment to flush out the ears and kill any eggs in the ears. A complete month of treatment is necessary to cure the mange.

Two other mites, less common in dogs, include *Dermanyssus gallinae* (the poultry or red mite) and *Eutrombicula alfreddugesi* (the North American mite associated with trombiculidiasis or chigger infestation). The poultry mite frequently lives on chickens, but can transfer to dogs who spend time near farm animals. Chigger infestation affects dogs in the central U.S. who have exposure to woodlands. The types of mange caused by both of these mites are treatable by veterinarians.

NOT A DROP TO DRINK

Never allow your dog to swim in polluted water or public areas where water quality can be suspect. Even perfectly clear water can harbor parasites, many of which can cause serious to fatal illnesses in canines. Areas inhabited by waterfowl and other wildlife are especially dangerous.

DO NOT MIX

Never mix parasite-control products without first consulting your vet. Some products can become toxic when combined with others and can cause fatal consequences.

INTERNAL PARASITES

Most animals—fishes, birds and mammals, including dogs and humans—have worms and other parasites that live inside their bodies. According to Dr. Herbert R. Axelrod, the fish pathologist, there are two kinds of parasites: dumb and smart. The smart parasites live in peaceful cooperation with their hosts (symbiosis), while the dumb parasites kill their hosts. Most worm infections are relatively easy to control. If they are not controlled, they weaken the host dog to the point that other medical problems occur, but they do not kill the host as dumb parasites would.

A brown dog tick, *Rhipicephalus sanguineus*, is an uncommon but annoying tick found on dogs.

Photo by Carolina Biological Supply/Phototake.

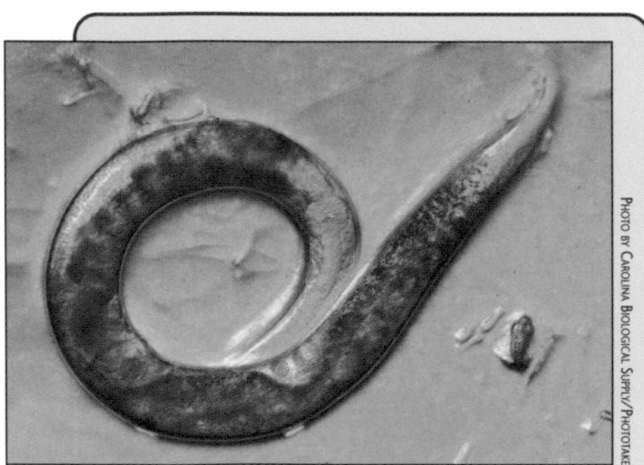

The roundworm *Rhabditis* can infect both dogs and humans.

ROUNDWORMS

Average-size dogs can pass 1,360,000 roundworm eggs every day. For example, if there were only 1 million dogs in the world, the world would be saturated with thousands of tons of dog feces. These feces would contain around 15,000,000,000 roundworm eggs.

Up to 31% of home yards and children's sand boxes in the US contain roundworm eggs.

Flushing dog's feces down the toilet is not a safe practice because the usual sewage treatments do not destroy roundworm eggs.

Infected puppies start shedding roundworm eggs at three weeks of age. They can be infected by their mother's milk.

The roundworm, *Ascaris lumbricoides.*

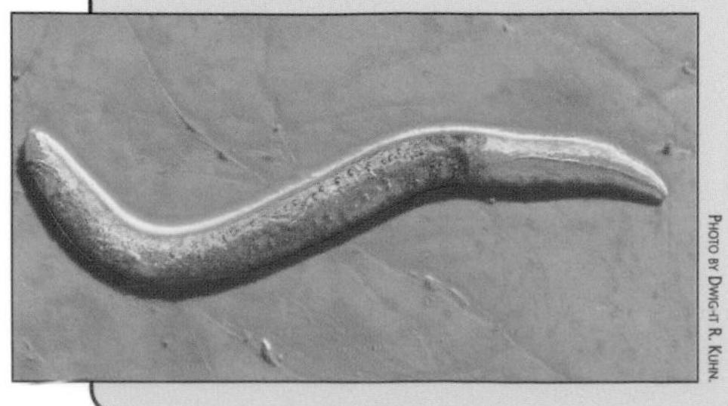

Roundworms

The roundworms that infect dogs are known scientifically as *Toxocara canis*. They live in the dog's intestines and shed eggs continually. It has been estimated that a dog produces about 6 or more ounces of feces every day. Each ounce of feces averages hundreds of thousands of roundworm eggs. There are no known areas in which dogs roam that do not contain roundworm eggs. The greatest danger of roundworms is that they infect people, too! It is wise to have your dog tested regularly for roundworms.

In young puppies, roundworms cause bloated bellies, diarrhea, coughing and vomiting, and are transmitted from the dam (through blood or milk). Affected puppies will not appear as animated as normal puppies. The worms appear spaghetti-like, measuring as long as 6 inches. Adult dogs can acquire roundworms through coprophagia (eating contaminated feces) or by killing rodents that carry roundworms.

Roundworm infection can kill puppies and cause severe problems in adults, as the hatched larvae travel to the lungs and trachea through the bloodstream. Cleanliness is the best preventative for roundworms. Always pick up after your dog and dispose of feces in appropriate receptacles.

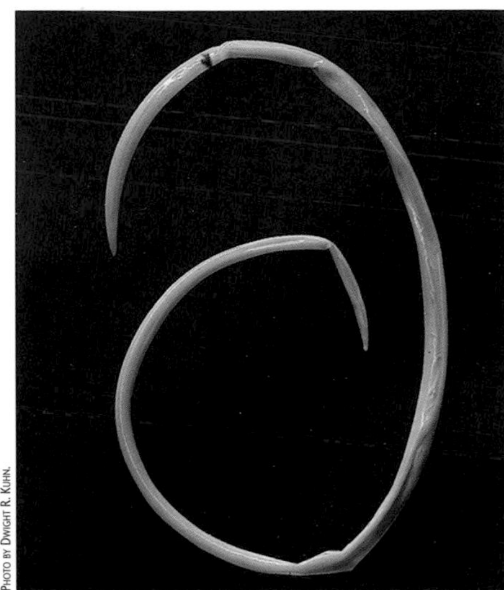

The hookworm, *Ancylostoma caninum.*

HOOKWORMS

In the United States, dog owners have to be concerned about four different species of hookworm, the most common and most serious of which is *Ancylostoma caninum,* which prefers warm climates. The others are *Ancylostoma braziliense, Ancylostoma tubaeforme* and *Uncinaria stenocephala,* the latter of which is a concern to dogs living in the northern U.S. and Canada, as this species prefers cold climates. Hookworms are dangerous to humans as well as to dogs and cats, and can be the cause of severe anemia due to iron deficiency. The worm uses its teeth to attach itself to the dog's intestines and changes the site of its attachment about six times per day. Each time the worm repositions itself, the dog loses blood and can become anemic. *Ancylostoma caninum* is the most likely of the four species to cause anemia in the dog.

Symptoms of hookworm infection include dark stools, weight loss, general weakness, pale coloration and anemia, as well as possible skin problems. Fortunately, hookworms are easily purged from the affected dog with a number of medications that have proven effective. Discuss these with your veterinarian. Most heartworm preventatives include a hookworm insecticide as well.

Owners also must be aware that hookworms can infect humans, who can acquire the larvae through exposure to contaminated feces. Since the worms cannot complete their life cycle on a human, the worms simply infest the skin and cause irritation. This condition is known as cutaneous larva migrans syndrome. As a preventative, use disposable gloves or a "poop-scoop" to pick up your dog's droppings and prevent your dog (or neighborhood cats) from defecating in children's play areas.

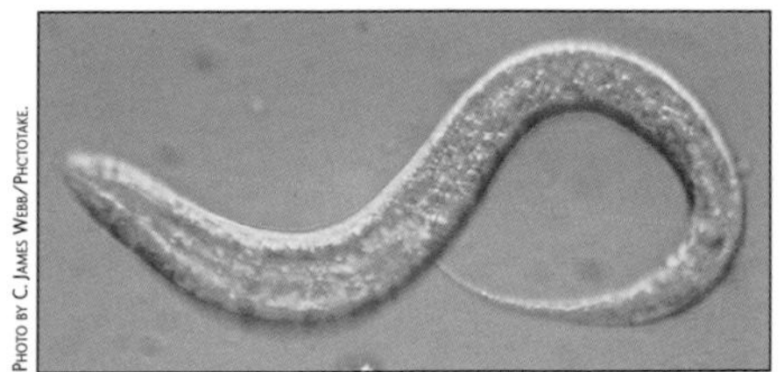

The infective stage of the hookworm larva.

TAPEWORMS

Humans, rats, squirrels, foxes, coyotes, wolves and domestic dogs are all susceptible to tapeworm infection. Except in humans, tapeworms are usually not a fatal infection. Infected individuals can harbor 1000 parasitic worms.

Tapeworms, like some other types of worm, are hermaphroditic, meaning male and female in the same worm.

If dogs eat infected rats or mice, or anything else infected with tapeworm, they get the tapeworm disease. One month after attaching to a dog's intestine, the worm starts shedding eggs. These eggs are infective immediately. Infective eggs can live for a few months without a host animal.

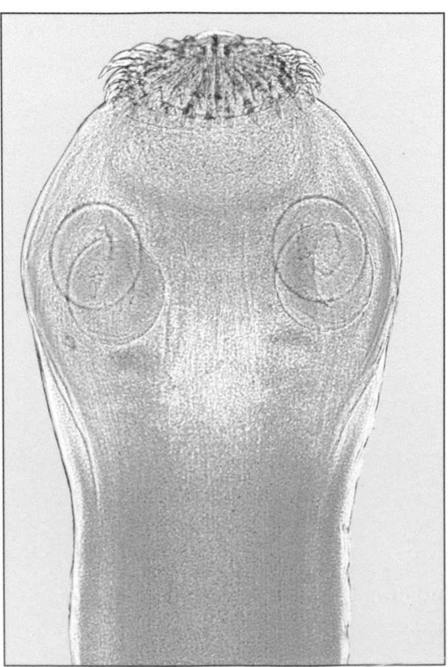

The head and rostellum (the round prominence on the scolex) of a tapeworm, which infects dogs and humans.

PHOTO BY CAROLINA BIOLOGICAL SUPPLY/PHOTOTAKE.

TAPEWORMS

There are many species of tapeworm, all of which are carried by fleas! The most common tapeworm affecting dogs is known as *Dipylidium caninum*. The dog eats the flea and starts the tapeworm cycle. Humans can also be infected with tapeworms—so don't eat fleas! Fleas are so small that your dog could pass them onto your hands, your plate or your food and thus make it possible for you to ingest a flea that is carrying tapeworm eggs.

While tapeworm infection is not life-threatening in dogs (smart parasite!), it can be the cause of a very serious liver disease for humans. About 50% of the humans infected with *Echinococcus multilocularis*, a type of tapeworm that causes alveolar hydatid, perish.

WHIPWORMS

In North America, whipworms are counted among the most common parasitic worms in dogs. The whipworm's scientific name is *Trichuris vulpis*. These worms attach themselves in the lower parts of the intestine, where they feed. Affected dogs may only experience upset tummies, colic and diarrhea. These worms, however, can live for months or years in the dog, beginning their larval stage in the small intestine, spending their adult stage in the large intestine and finally passing infective eggs through the dog's feces. The only way to detect whipworms is through a fecal examination, though this is not always foolproof. Treatment for whipworms is tricky, due to the worms' unusual life-cycle pattern, and very often dogs are reinfected due to exposure to infective eggs on the ground. The whipworm eggs can survive in the environment for as long as five years, thus cleaning up droppings in your own backyard as well as in public places is absolutely essential for sanitation purposes and the health of your dog and others.

THREADWORMS

Though less common than roundworms, hookworms and those previously discussed, threadworms concern dog owners in the southwestern U.S. and Gulf Coast area, where the climate is hot and humid. Living in the small intestine of the dog, this worm measures a mere 2 millimeters and is round in shape. Like that of the whipworm, the threadworm's life cycle is very complex and the eggs and larvae are passed through the feces. A deadly disease in humans, *Strongyloides* readily infects people, and the handling of feces is the most common means of transmission. Threadworms are most often seen in young puppies; bloody diarrhea and pneumonia are symptoms. Sick puppies must be isolated and treated immediately; vets recommend a follow-up treatment one month later.

HEARTWORM PREVENTATIVES

There are many heartworm preventatives on the market, many of which are sold at your veterinarian's office. These products can be given daily or monthly, depending on the manufacturer's instructions. All of these preventatives contain chemical insecticides directed at killing heartworms, which leads to some controversy among dog owners. In effect, heartworm preventatives are necessary evils, though you should determine how necessary based on your pet's lifestyle. There is no doubt that heartworm is a dreadful disease that threatens the lives of dogs. However, the likelihood of your dog's being bitten by an infected mosquito is slim in most places, and a mosquito-repellent (or an herbal remedy such as Wormwood or Black Walnut) is much safer for your dog and will not compromise his immune system (the way heartworm preventatives will). Should you decide to use the traditional preventative "medications," you can consider giving the pill every other or third month. Since the toxins in the pill will kill the heartworms at all stages of development, the pill would be effective in killing larvae, nymphs or adults and it takes four months for the larvae to reach the adult stage. Thus, there is no rationale to poisoning the dog's system on a monthly basis. Lastly, do not give the pill during the winter months since there are no mosquitoes around to pass on their infection, unless you live in a tropical environment.

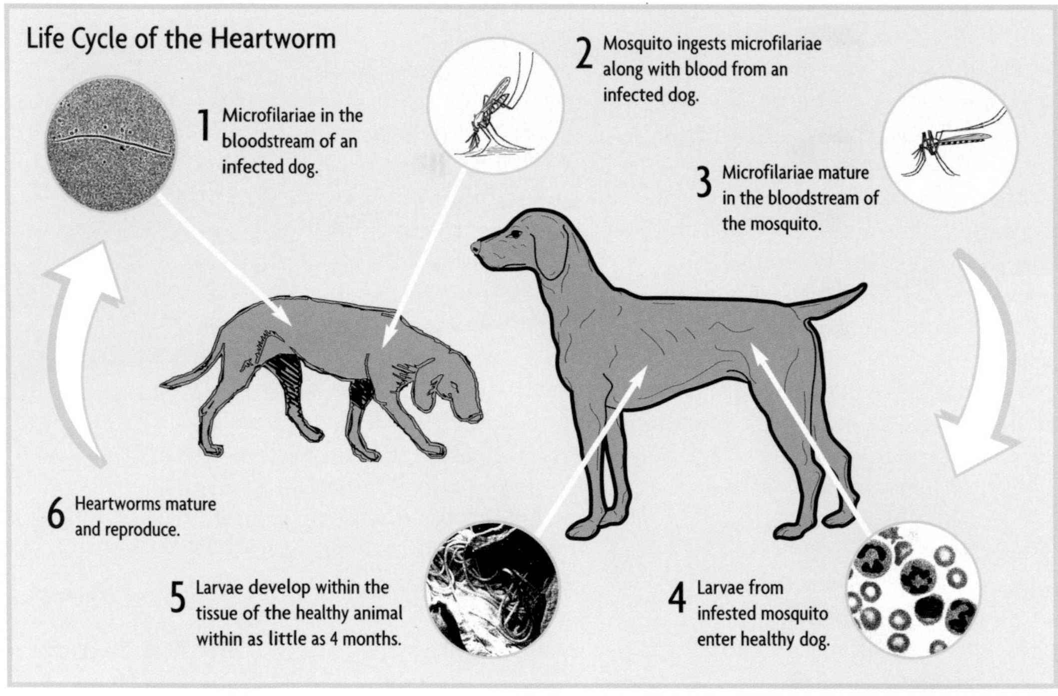

HEARTWORMS

Heartworms are thin, extended worms up to 12 inches long, which live in a dog's heart and the major blood vessels surrounding it. Dogs may have up to 200 worms. Symptoms may be loss of energy, loss of appetite, coughing, the development of a pot belly and anemia.

Heartworms are transmitted by mosquitoes. The mosquito drinks the blood of an infected dog and takes in larvae with the blood. The larvae, called microfilariae, develop within the body of the mosquito and are passed on to the next dog bitten after the larvae mature. It takes two to three weeks for the larvae to develop to the infective stage within the body of the mosquito. Dogs are usually treated at about six weeks of age and maintained on a prophylactic dose given monthly.

Blood testing for heartworms is not necessarily indicative of how seriously your dog is infected. Although this is a dangerous disease, it is not easy for a dog to be infected. Discuss the various preventatives with your vet, as there are many different types now available. Together you can decide on a safe course of prevention for your dog.

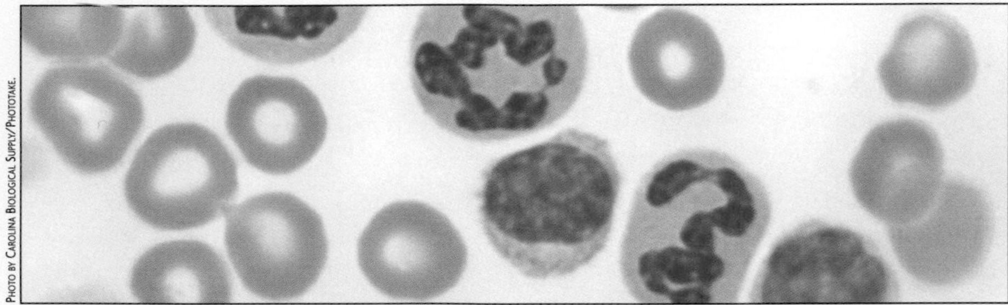

Photo by Carolina Biological Supply/Phototake.

Magnified heartworm larvae, *Dirofilaria immitis.*

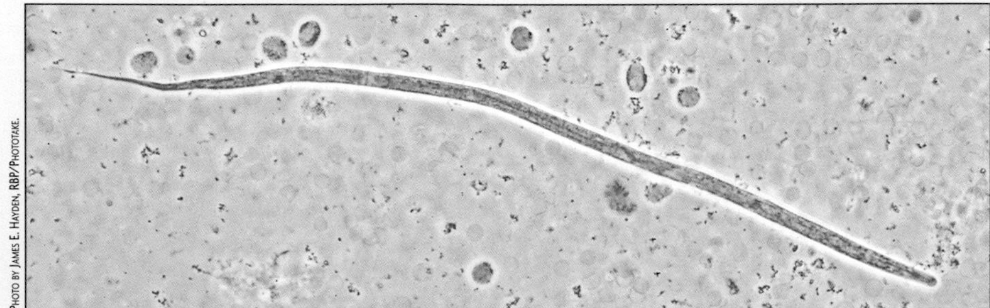

Photo by James E. Hayden, RBP/Phototake.

Heartworm, *Dirofilaria immitis.*

Photo by James E. Hayden, RPB/Phototake.

The heart of a dog infected with canine heartworm, *Dirofilaria immitis.*

HOMEOPATHY:
an alternative to conventional medicine

"Less is Most"

Using this principle, the strength of a homeopathic remedy is measured by the number of serial dilutions that were undertaken to create it. The greater the number of serial dilutions, the greater the strength of the homeopathic remedy. The potency of a remedy that has been made by making a dilution of 1 part in 100 parts (or 1/100) is 1c or 1cH. If this remedy is subjected to a series of further dilutions, each one being 1/100, a more dilute and stronger remedy is produced. If the remedy is diluted in this way six times, it is called 6c or 6cH. A dilution of 6c is 1 part in 1000,000,000,000. In general, higher potencies in more frequent doses are better for acute symptoms and lower potencies in more infrequent doses are more useful for chronic, long-standing problems.

CURING OUR DOGS NATURALLY

Holistic medicine means treating the whole animal as a unique, perfect living being. Generally, holistic treatments do not suppress the symptoms that the body naturally produces, as do most medications prescribed by conventional doctors and vets. Holistic methods seek to cure disease by regaining balance and harmony in the patient's environment. Some of these methods include use of nutritional therapy, herbs, flower essences, aromatherapy, acupuncture, massage, chiropractic and, of course, the most popular holistic approach, homeopathy. Homeopathy is a theory or system of treating illness with small doses of substances which, if administered in larger quantities, would produce the symptoms that the patient already has. This approach is often described as "like cures like." Although modern veterinary medicine is geared toward the "quick fix," homeopathy relies on the belief that, given the time, the body is able to heal itself and return to its natural, healthy state.

Choosing a remedy to cure a problem in our dogs is the difficult part of homeopathy. Consult with your veterinarian for a professional diagnosis of your dog's symptoms. Often these symptoms require immediate conventional care. If your vet is willing, and somewhat knowledgeable, you may attempt a homeopathic remedy. Be aware that cortisone prevents homeopathic remedies from working. There are hundreds of possibilities and combinations to cure many problems in dogs, from basic physical problems such as excessive shedding, fleas or other parasites, unattractive doggy odor, bad breath, upset tummy, obesity, dry, oily or dull coat, diarrhea, ear problems or eye discharge (including tears and dry or mucusy matter), to behavioral abnormalities, such as fear of loud noises, habitual licking, poor appetite, excessive barking and various phobias. From alumina to zincum metallicum, the remedies span the planet and the imagination…from flowers and weeds to chemicals, insect droppings, diesel smoke and volcanic ash.

Using "Like to Treat Like"

Unlike conventional medicines that suppress symptoms, homeopathic remedies treat illnesses with small doses of substances that, if administered in larger quantities, would produce the symptoms that the patient already has. While the same homeopathic remedy can be used to treat different symptoms in different dogs, here are some interesting remedies and their uses.

Apis Mellifica
(made from honey bee venom) can be used for allergies or to reduce swelling that occurs in acutely infected kidneys.

Diesel Smoke
can be used to help control travel sickness.

Calcarea Fluorica
(made from calcium fluoride, which helps harden bone structure) can be useful in treating hard lumps in tissues.

Natrum Muriaticum
(made from common salt, sodium chloride) is useful in treating thin, thirsty dogs.

Nitricum Acidum
(made from nitric acid) is used for symptoms you would expect to see from contact with acids such as lesions, especially where the skin joins the linings of body orifices or openings such as the lips and nostrils.

Symphytum
(made from the herb knitbone, *Symphytum officianale*) is used to encourage bones to heal.

Urtica Urens
(made from the common stinging nettle) is used in treating painful, irritating rashes.

HOMEOPATHIC REMEDIES FOR YOUR DOG

Symptom/Ailment	Possible Remedy
ALLERGIES	Apis Mellifica 30c, Astacus Fluviatilis 6c, Pulsatilla 30c, Urtica Urens 6c
ALOPECIA	Alumina 30c, Lycopodium 30c, Sepia 30c, Thallium 6c
ANAL GLANDS (BLOCKED)	Hepar Sulphuris Calcareum 30c, Sanicula 6c, Silicea 6c
ARTHRITIS	Rhus Toxicodendron 6c, Bryonia Alba 6c
CATARACT	Calcarea Carbonica 6c, Conium Maculatum 6c, Phosphorus 30c, Silicea 30c
CONSTIPATION	Alumina 6c, Carbo Vegetabilis 30c, Graphites 6c, Nitricum Acidum 30c, Silicea 6c
COUGHING	Aconitum Napellus 6c, Belladonna 30c, Hyoscyamus Niger 30c, Phosphorus 30c
DIARRHEA	Arsenicum Album 30c, Aconitum Napellus 6c, Chamomilla 30c, Mercurius Corrosivus 30c
DRY EYE	Zincum Metallicum 30c
EAR PROBLEMS	Aconitum Napellus 30c, Belladonna 30c, Hepar Sulphuris 30c, Tellurium 30c, Psorinum 200c
EYE PROBLEMS	Borax 6c, Aconitum Napellus 30c, Graphites 6c, Staphysagria 6c, Thuja Occidentalis 30c
GLAUCOMA	Aconitum Napellus 30c, Apis Mellifica 6c, Phosphorus 30c
HEAT STROKE	Belladonna 30c, Gelsemium Sempervirens 30c, Sulphur 30c
HICCUPS	Cinchona Deficinalis 6c
HIP DYSPLASIA	Colocynthis 6c, Rhus Toxicodendron 6c, Bryonia Alba 6c
INCONTINENCE	Argentum Nitricum 6c, Causticum 30c, Conium Maculatum 30c, Pulsatilla 30c, Sepia 30c
INSECT BITES	Apis Mellifica 30c, Cantharis 30c, Hypericum Perforatum 6c, Urtica Urens 30c
ITCHING	Alumina 30c, Arsenicum Album 30c, Carbo Vegetabilis 30c, Hypericum Perforatum 6c, Mezerium 6c, Sulphur 30c
KENNEL COUGH	Drosera 6c, Ipecacuanha 30c
MASTITIS	Apis Mellifica 30c, Belladonna 30c, Urtica Urens 1m
MOTION SICKNESS	Cocculus 6c, Petroleum 6c
PATELLAR LUXATION	Gelsemium Sempervirens 6c, Rhus Toxicodendron 6c
PENIS PROBLEMS	Aconitum Napellus 30c, Hepar Sulphuris Calcareum 30c, Pulsatilla 30c, Thuja Occidentalis 6c
PUPPY TEETHING	Calcarea Carbonica 6c, Chamomilla 6c, Phytolacca 6c

YOUR SENIOR
DOBERMAN PINSCHER

The term *old* is a qualitative term, so for dogs, as well as for their masters, old is relative. Certainly we can all distinguish between a puppy Doberman Pinscher and an adult Doberman Pinscher—there are the obvious physical traits, such as size, appearance and facial expressions, and personality traits. Puppies and young dogs like to play with children. Children's natural exuberance is a good match for the seemingly endless energy of young dogs. They like to run, jump, chase and retrieve. When dogs grow up and cease their interaction with children, they are often thought of as being too old to play with the kids. On the other hand, if a Doberman Pinscher is only exposed to people with quieter lifestyles, his life will normally be less active and the decrease in his activity level as he ages will not be as obvious.

If people live to be 100 years old, dogs live to be 20 years old. While this sounds like a good rule of thumb, it is very inaccurate. When trying to compare dog years to human years, you cannot make a generalization about all dogs. You can make the generalization that 10 years is a good lifespan for a Doberman Pinscher, but some Doberman Pinschers have been known to live to 15 years. Dogs are generally considered mature within three years, but they can reproduce even earlier. So the first three years of a dog's life are like seven times that of comparable humans. That means a 3-year-old dog is like a 21-year-old human. As the curve of comparison shows, there is no hard and fast rule for comparing dog and human ages. The comparison is made even more difficult, for not

OLD-DOG DAYS

The bottom line is simply that your dog is getting old when you think he is getting old because he slows down in his general activities, including walking, running, eating, jumping and retrieving. On the other hand, certain activities increase, such as more sleeping, more barking and more repetition of habits like going to the door without being called when you put your coat on to leave or go outdoors.

WHEN YOUR DOG GETS OLD... SIGNS THE OWNER CAN LOOK FOR

IF YOU NOTICE...	IT COULD INDICATE...
Discoloration of teeth and gums, foul breath, loss of appetite	Abcesses, gum disease, mouth lesions
Lumps, bumps, cysts, warts, fatty tumors	Cancers, benign or malignant
Cloudiness of eyes, apparent loss of sight	Cataracts, lenticular sclerosis, PRA, retinal dysplasia, blindness
Flaky coat, alopecia (hair loss)	Hormonal problems, hypothyroidism
Obesity, appetite loss, excessive weight gain	Various problems
Household accidents, increased urination	Diabetes, kidney or bladder disease
Increased thirst	Kidney disease, diabetes mellitus
Change in sleeping habits, coughing	Heart disease
Difficulty moving	Arthritis, degenerative joint disease, spondylosis (degenerative spine disease)

IF YOU NOTICE ANY OF THESE SIGNS, AN APPOINTMENT SHOULD BE MADE IMMEDIATELY WITH A VET FOR A THOROUGH EVALUATION.

Gray hair on the muzzle is one of the first recognizable signs of a dog's aging.

The older dog's activity level will noticeably decrease.

CDS
COGNITIVE DYSFUNCTION SYNDROME
"Old-Dog Syndrome"

SYMPTOMS OF CDS

There are many ways to evaluate old-dog syndrome. Vets have defined CDS (cognitive dysfunction syndrome) as the gradual deterioration of cognitive abilities. These are indicated by changes in the dog's behavior. When a dog changes his routine response, and maladies have been eliminated as the cause of these behavioral changes, then CDS is the usual diagnosis.

More than half the dogs over eight years old suffer from some form of CDS. The older the dog, the more chance he has of suffering from CDS. In humans, doctors often dismiss the CDS behavioral changes as part of "winding down."

There are four major signs of CDS: frequent potty accidents inside the home, sleeping much more or much less than normal, acting confused and failing to respond to social stimuli.

FREQUENT POTTY ACCIDENTS

- ***Urinates in the house.***
- ***Defecates in the house.***
- ***Doesn't signal that he wants to go out.***

SLEEP PATTERNS

- ***Moves much more slowly.***
- ***Sleeps more than normal during the day.***
- ***Sleeps less during the night.***

CONFUSION

- ***Goes outside and just stands there.***
- ***Appears confused with a faraway look in his eyes.***
- ***Hides more often.***
- ***Doesn't recognize friends.***
- ***Doesn't come when called.***
- ***Walks around listlessly and without a destination goal.***

FAILURE TO RESPOND TO SOCIAL STIMULI

- ***Comes to people less frequently, whether called or not.***
- ***Doesn't tolerate petting for more than a short time.***
- ***Doesn't come to the door when you return home from work.***

all humans age at the same rate...and human females live longer than human males.

WHAT TO LOOK FOR IN SENIORS

Most veterinarians and behaviorists use the seven-year mark as the time to consider a dog a "senior." The term *senior* does not imply that the dog is geriatric and has begun to fail in mind and body. Aging is essentially a slowing process. Humans readily admit that they feel a difference in their activity level from age 20 to 30, and then from 30 to 40, etc. By treating the seven-year-old dog as a senior, owners are able to implement certain therapeutic and preventative medical strategies with the help of their vets. A senior-care program should include at least two veterinary visits per year, screening sessions to determine the dog's health status, as well as nutritional counseling. Veterinarians determine the senior dog's health status through a blood smear for a complete blood count, serum chemistry profile with electrolytes, urinalysis, blood pressure check, electrocardiogram, ocular tonometry (pressure on the eyeball), and dental prophylaxis.

Such an extensive program for senior dogs is well advised before owners start to see the obvious physical signs of aging, such as slower and inhibited movement, graying, increased sleep/nap periods, and disinterest in play and other activity. This preventative

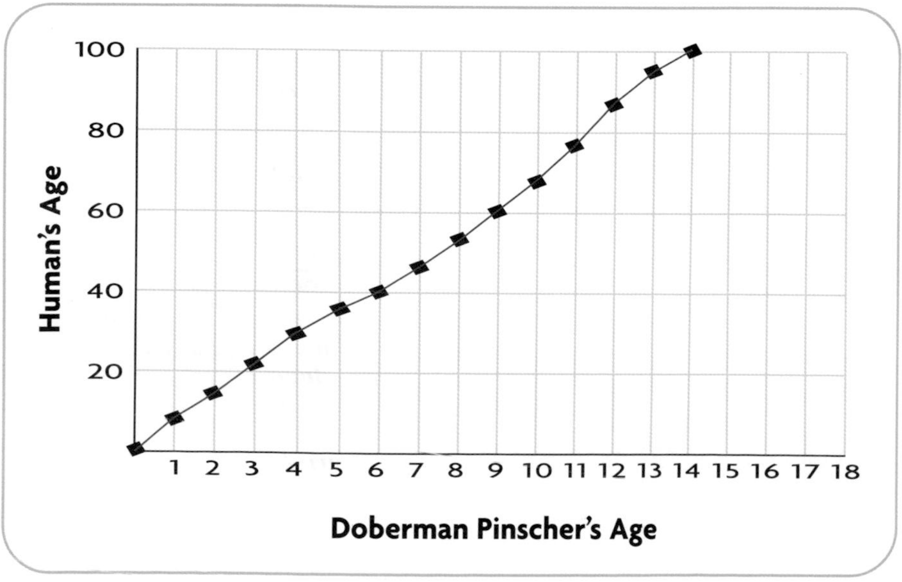

No two dogs age at the same rate. Each dog is an individual. Have your vet perform an evaluation of your Doberman Pinscher at around seven years of age.

program promises a longer, healthier life for the aging dog. Among the physical problems common in aging dogs are the loss of sight and hearing, arthritis, kidney and liver failure, diabetes mellitus, heart disease, and Cushing's disease (a hormonal disease).

In addition to the physical manifestations discussed, there are some behavioral changes and problems related to aging dogs. Dogs suffering from hearing or vision loss, dental discomfort or arthritis can become aggressive. Likewise the near-deaf and/or blind dog may be startled more easily and react in an unexpectedly aggressive manner. Seniors suffering from senility can become more impatient and irritable. Housesoiling accidents are associated with loss of mobility, kidney problems, loss of sphincter control as well as plaque accumulation, physiological brain changes and reactions to medications. Older dogs, just like young puppies, suffer from separation anxiety, which can lead to excessive barking, whining, housesoiling and destructive behavior. Seniors may become fearful of everyday sounds, such as vacuum cleaners, heaters, thunder and passing traffic. Some dogs have difficulty sleeping, due to discomfort, the need for frequent potty visits and the like.

Owners should avoid spoiling the older dog with too many fatty treats. Obesity is a common problem in older dogs and subtracts years from their lives. Keep the senior dog as trim as possible since excess weight puts additional stress on the body's vital organs. Some breeders recommend supplementing the diet with foods high in fiber and lower in calories. Adding fresh vegetables and marrow broth to the senior's diet makes a tasty, low-calorie, low-fat supplement. Vets also offer specialty diets for senior dogs that are worth exploring.

Your dog, as he nears his twilight years, needs his owner's patience and good care more than ever. Never punish an older dog for an accident or abnormal behavior. For all the years of love, protection and companionship that your dog has provided, he deserves special attention and courtesies. The older dog may need to relieve himself at 3 a.m. because he can no longer hold it for eight hours. Older dogs may not be able to remain crated for more than two or three hours. It may be time to give up a sofa or chair to your old friend. Although he may not seem as enthusiastic about your attention and petting, he does appreciate the considerations you offer as he gets older.

Your Doberman Pinscher does not understand why his world is slowing down. Owners must make the transition into the golden years as pleasant and rewarding as possible.

SIGNS OF AGING

The symptoms listed below are symptoms that gradually appear and become more noticeable. They are not life-threatening; however, the symptoms below are to be taken very seriously and a discussion with your veterinarian is warranted:

- Your dog cries and whimpers when he moves and stops running completely.
- Convulsions start or become more serious and frequent. The usual convulsion (spasm) is when the dog stiffens and starts to tremble, being unable or unwilling to move. The seizure usually lasts for 5 to 30 minutes.
- Your dog drinks more water and urinates more frequently. Wetting and bowel accidents take place indoors without warning.
- Vomiting becomes more and more frequent.

WHAT TO DO WHEN THE TIME COMES

You are never fully prepared to make a rational decision about putting your dog to sleep. It is very obvious that you love your Doberman Pinscher or you would not be reading this book. Putting a loved dog to sleep is extremely difficult. It is a decision that must be made with your vet. You are usually forced to make the decision when one or more life-threatening symptoms become serious enough for you to seek veterinary help.

If the prognosis of the malady indicates that the end is near and your beloved pet will only suffer and experience no enjoyment for the balance of his life, then euthanasia is the right choice.

What Is Euthanasia?

Euthanasia derives from the Greek, meaning *good death*. In other words, it means the planned, painless killing of a dog suffering from a painful, incurable condition, or who is so aged that he cannot walk, see, eat or control his excretory functions.

Euthanasia is usually accomplished by injection with an overdose of an anesthesia or barbiturate. Aside from the prick of the needle, the experience is usually painless.

Making the Decision

The decision to euthanize your dog is never easy. The days during which the dog becomes ill and the end occurs can be unusually stressful for you. If this is your first experience with the death of a loved one, you may need the comfort dictated by your religious beliefs. If you are the head of the family and have children, you should involve them in the decision of putting your Doberman Pinscher to sleep. Usually your dog can be maintained on drugs for a few days while he is kept in the clinic in order to give you ample time to make a decision. During this time, talking with members of the family or religious representatives, or even people who have lived through this same experience, can ease the burden of your inevitable decision. In any case, euthanasia is painful and stressful for the family of the dog.

EUTHANASIA SERVICES

Euthanasia must be done by a licensed veterinarian. There also may be societies for the prevention of cruelty to animals in your area. They often offer this service upon a vet's recommendation.

The Final Resting Place

Dogs can have many of the same privileges as humans. Your dog can be buried in a pet cemetery, buried in your yard in a place suitably marked with a stone, newly planted tree or bush or cremated with the ashes being given to you.

All of these options should be discussed frankly and openly with your vet. Do not be afraid to ask financial questions. Mass cremations are less expensive, but the ashes you get may not be only the ashes of your beloved dog. If you want a private cremation, there are small crematoriums available to all veterinary clinics. Your vet can usually arrange for this but it may be a little more expensive. Your vet also can help you locate a pet cemetery if you choose this option.

Getting Another Dog?

The grief of losing your beloved dog will be as lasting as the grief of losing a human friend or relative. In most cases, if your dog died of old age (if there is such a thing), he had slowed down considerably. Do you want a new Doberman Pinscher puppy to replace him? Or are you better off finding a more mature Doberman Pinscher, say two to three years of age, which will usually be housetrained and will have an already developed personality. In this case, you can find out if you like each other after a few hours of being together.

The decision is, of course, your own. Do you want another Doberman Pinscher? Perhaps you want a smaller or larger dog? How much do you want to spend on a dog? Look in your local newspapers for advertisements, or, better yet, consult your local society for the prevention of cruelty to animals to adopt a dog. It is harder to find puppies at an animal shelter, but there are often many adult dogs in need of good homes. You may be able to find another Doberman Pinscher, or you may choose another breed or a mixed-breed dog. Most people usually stay with the same breed because they know and love the characteristics of that breed. Then, too, they often know people who have the same breed and perhaps they are lucky enough that a breeder they know and respect expects a litter soon. What could be better?

Consult your vet to help you locate a pet cemetery in your area.

SHOWING YOUR
DOBERMAN PINSCHER

When you purchase your Doberman Pinscher, you will make it clear to the breeder whether you want one just as a lovable companion and pet, or if you hope to be buying a Doberman Pinscher with show prospects. No reputable breeder will sell you a young puppy and tell you that it is *definitely* of show quality, for so much can go wrong during the early months of a puppy's development. If you plan to show, what you will hopefully have acquired is a puppy with "show potential."

Consider trying your hand at showing your Doberman Pinscher. The show fancy welcomes novices with open arms!

To the novice, exhibiting a Doberman Pinscher in the show ring may look easy, but it takes a lot of hard work and devotion to do top winning at a show such as the prestigious Westminster Kennel Club dog show, not to mention a little luck too!

The first concept that the canine novice learns when watching a dog show is that each dog first competes against members of his own breed. Once the judge has selected the best member of each breed (Best of Breed), provided that the show is judged on a Group system, that chosen dog will compete with other dogs in his group. Finally, the dogs chosen first in each group will compete for Best in Show.

The second concept that you must understand is that the dogs are not actually compared against one another. The judge compares each dog against his breed standard, the written description of the ideal specimen that is approved by the American Kennel Club (AKC). While some early breed standards were indeed based on specific dogs that were famous or popular, many dedicated enthusiasts say that a perfect specimen, as described in the standard, has never walked into a show ring, has never been bred and, to the woe of dog breeders around the globe, does not exist. Breeders attempt to get as close to this ideal as possible with every litter, but theoretically the "perfect" dog is so elusive that it is impossible. (And if the "perfect" dog were born, breeders and judges would never agree that it was indeed "perfect.")

If you are interested in exploring the world of dog showing, your best bet is to join your local breed club or the national parent club, which is the Doberman Pinscher Club of America. These clubs often host both regional and national specialties, shows only for Doberman Pinschers, which can include conformation as well as obedience and agility trials. Even if you have no intention of competing with your Doberman Pinscher, a specialty is like a festival for lovers of the breed who congregate to share their favorite topic: Doberman Pinschers! Clubs also send out newsletters, and some organize training days and seminars in order that people may learn more about their chosen

A Best in Show Doberman! What could be more exciting than winning the top award at a dog show?

BECOMING A CHAMPION

An official AKC champion of record requires that a dog accumulate 15 points under three different judges, including two "majors" under different judges. Points are awarded based on the number of dogs entered into competition, varying from breed to breed and place to place. A win of three, four or five points is considered a "major." The AKC annually assigns a schedule of points to adjust the variations that accompany a breed's popularity and the population of a given area.

breed. To locate the breed club closest to you, contact the American Kennel Club, which furnishes the rules and regulations for all of these events plus general dog registration and other basic requirements of dog ownership.

The American Kennel Club offers three kinds of conformation shows: an all-breed show (for all AKC-recognized breeds), a specialty show (for one breed only, usually sponsored by the parent club) and a Group show (for all breeds in the group).

For a dog to become an AKC champion of record, the dog must accumulate 15 points at the shows from at least three different judges, including two "majors." A "major" is defined as a three-, four- or five-point win, and the number of points per win is determined by the number of dogs entered in the show on the day. Depending on the breed, the number of points that are awarded varies. In a breed as popular as the Doberman Pinscher, more dogs are needed to rack up the points. At any dog show, only one dog and one bitch of each breed can win points.

Dog showing does not offer "co-ed" classes. Dogs and bitches never compete against each other in the classes. Non-champion dogs are called "class dogs" because they compete in one of five classes. Dogs are entered in a particular class depending on their age and previous show wins. To begin, there is the Puppy Class (for 6- to 9-month-olds and for 9- to 12-month-olds); this class is followed by the Novice Class (for dogs that have not won any first prizes except in the Puppy Class or three first prizes in the Novice Class and have not accumulated any points toward their champion title); the Bred-by-Exhibitor Class (for dogs handled by their breeders or handled by one of the breeder's immediate family); the American-bred Class (for dogs bred in the U.S.!) and the Open Class (for any dog that is not a champion).

MEET THE AKC

The American Kennel Club is the main governing body of the dog sport in the United States. Founded in 1884, the AKC consists of 500 or more independent dog clubs plus 4,500 affiliate clubs, all of which follow the AKC rules and regulations. Additionally, the AKC maintains a registry for pure-bred dogs in the U.S. and works to preserve the integrity of the sport and its continuation in the country. Over 1,000,000 dogs are registered each year, representing about 150 recognized breeds. There are over 15,000 competitive events held annually for which over 2,000,000 dogs enter to participate. Dogs compete to earn over 40 different titles, from Champion to Companion Dog to Master Agility Champion.

Competition at dog shows is often steep. Your careful selection, training and conditioning will pay off grandly if your dog is chosen as Best of Breed.

The judge at the show begins judging the Puppy Class, first dogs and then bitches, and proceeds through the classes. The judge places his winners first through fourth in each class. In the Winners Class, the first-place winners of each class compete with one another to determine Winners Dog and Winners Bitch. The judge also places a Reserve Winners Dog and Reserve Winners Bitch, which could be awarded the points in the case of a disqualification. The Winners Dog and Winners Bitch, the two that are awarded the points for the breed, then compete with any champions of record entered in the show. The judge reviews the Winners Dog, Winners Bitch and all the champions (often called "specials") to select his Best of Breed. The Best of Winners is selected between the Winners Dog and Winners Bitch. Were one of these two to be selected Best of Breed, he or she would automatically be named Best of Winners as well. Finally the judge selects his Best of Opposite Sex to the Best of Breed winner.

At a Group show or all-breed show, the Best of Breed winners from each breed then compete against one another for Group One through Group Four. The judge compares each Best of Breed to his breed standard, and the dog that most closely lives up to the ideal for his breed is selected as Group One. Finally, all seven group winners (from the Working Group, Toy Group, Hound Group, etc.) compete for Best in Show.

To find out about dog shows in your area, you can subscribe to the American Kennel Club's monthly magazine, the *American Kennel Gazette* and the accompanying *Events Calendar*. You can also look in your local newspaper for advertisements for dog shows in your area or go on the Internet to the AKC's website, www.akc.org.

If your Doberman Pinscher is six months of age or older and registered with the AKC, you can enter him in a dog show where the breed is offered classes.

FIVE CLASSES AT SHOWS

At most AKC all-breed shows, there are five regular classes offered: Puppy, Novice, Bred-by-Exhibitor, American-bred and Open. The Puppy Class is usually divided as six to nine months of age and nine to twelve months of age. When deciding in which class to enter your dog, male or female, you must carefully check the show schedule to make sure that you have selected the right class. Depending on the age of the dog, previous first-place wins and the sex of the dog, you must make the best choice. It is possible to enter a one-year-old dog who has not won sufficient first places in any of the non-Puppy Classes, though the competition is more intense the further you progress from the Puppy Class.

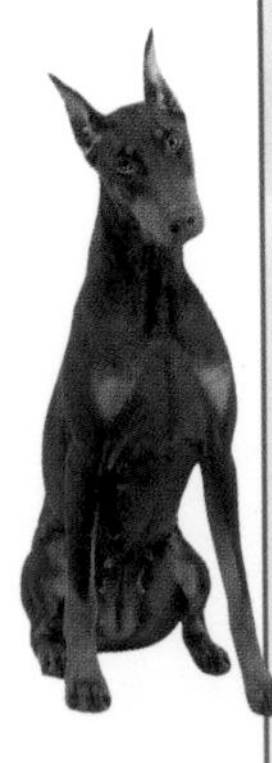

Provided that your Doberman Pinscher does not have a disqualifying fault, he can compete. Only unaltered dogs can be entered in a dog show, so if you have spayed or neutered your Doberman Pinscher, your dog cannot compete in conformation shows. The reason for this is simple. Dog shows are the main forum to prove which representatives of a breed are worthy of being bred. Only dogs that have achieved championships—the AKC "seal of approval" for quality in pure-bred dogs—should be bred. Altered dogs, however, can participate in other AKC events such as obedience trials and the Canine Good Citizen program.

ENTERING A DOG SHOW

Before you actually step into the ring, you would be well advised to sit back and observe the judge's ring procedure. If it is your first time in the ring, stand back and study how the exhibitor in front of you is performing. The judge asks each handler to "stack" the dog, hopefully showing the dog off to his best advantage. The judge will observe the dog from a distance and from different angles, and approach the dog to check his teeth, overall structure, alertness and muscle tone, as well as consider how well the dog "conforms" to the standard. Most importantly, the judge will have the exhibitor move the dog around the ring in some pattern that he should specify (always listen since some judges change their directions—and the judge is always right!). Finally, the judge will give the dog one last look before moving on to the next exhibitor.

If you are not in the top four in your class at your first show, do not be discouraged. Be patient and consistent, and you may eventually find yourself in a winning line-up. Remember that the winners were once in your shoes and have devoted many hours and much money to earn the placement. If you find that your dog is losing every time and never getting a nod, it may be time to consider a different dog sport or to just enjoy your Doberman Pinscher as a pet. Parent clubs offer other events, such as agility, tracking, obedience, Schutzhund, instinct tests and more, which may be of interest to the owner of a well-trained Doberman Pinscher.

CANINE GOOD CITIZEN® PROGRAM

Have you ever considered getting your dog "certified"? The AKC's Canine Good Citizen® Program affords your dog just that opportunity. Your dog shows that he is a well-behaved canine citizen, using the basic training and good manners you have taught him, by taking a series of ten tests that illustrate that he can behave properly at home, in a public place and around other dogs. The tests are administered by participating dog clubs, colleges, 4-H clubs, scouts and other community groups and are open to all pure-bred and mixed-breed dogs. Upon passing the ten tests, the suffix CGC is then applied to your dog's name.

The ten tests are: 1. Accepting a friendly stranger; 2. Sitting politely for petting; 3. Appearance and grooming; 4. Walking on a lead; 5. Walking through a group of people; 6. Sit, down and stay on command; 7. Coming when called; 8. Meeting another dog; 9. Calm reaction to distractions; 10. Separation from owner.

At obedience trials, dogs entered in the Open Class are required to retrieve the dumbbell.

OBEDIENCE TRIALS

Obedience trials in the U.S. trace back to the early 1930s when organized obedience training was developed to demonstrate how well dog and owner could work together. The pioneer of obedience trials is Mrs. Helen Whitehouse Walker, a Standard Poodle fancier, who designed a series of exercises after the Associated Sheep, Police Army Dog Society of Great Britain. Since the days of Mrs. Walker, obedience trials have grown by leaps and bounds, and today there are over 2,000 trials held in the U.S. every year, with more than 100,000 dogs competing. Any AKC-registered dog can enter an obedience trial, regardless of conformational disqualifications or neutering.

Obedience trials are divided into three levels of progressive difficulty. At the first level, the Novice, dogs compete for the title Companion Dog (CD); at the intermediate level, the Open, dogs compete for the title Companion Dog Excellent (CDX); and at the advanced level, the Utility, dogs compete for the title Utility Dog (UD). Classes are sub-divided into "A" (for beginners) and "B" (for more experienced handlers). A perfect score at any level is 200, and a dog must score 170 or better to earn a "leg," of which three are needed to earn the title. To earn points, the dog must score more than 50% of the available points in each exercise; the possible points range from 20 to 40.

Each level consists of a different set of exercises. In the Novice level, the dog must heel on- and off-lead, come, long sit, long down and stand for examination. These skills are the basic ones required for a well-behaved "Companion Dog." The Open level requires that the dog perform the same exercises above but without a leash for extended lengths of time, as well as retrieve a dumbbell, broad jump and drop on recall. In the Utility level, dogs must perform ten difficult exercises, including scent discrimination, hand signals for basic commands, directed jump and directed retrieve.

Once a dog has earned the UD title, he can compete with other proven obedience dogs for the coveted title of Utility Dog Excel-

INFORMATION ON CLUBS

You can get information about dog shows from the national kennel clubs:

American Kennel Club
5580 Centerview Dr., Raleigh, NC 27606-3390
www.akc.org

United Kennel Club
100 E. Kilgore Road, Kalamazoo, MI 49002
www.ukcdogs.com

Canadian Kennel Club
89 Skyway Ave., Suite 100, Etobicoke, Ontario
M9W 6R4 Canada
www.ckc.ca

The Kennel Club
1-5 Clarges St., Piccadilly, London W1Y 8AB UK
www.the-kennel-club.org.uk

Doberman Pinschers are natural jumpers and excel in the high jump at agility trials. Few canine competitions can compare to the excitement and energy of an agility trial.

lent (UDX), which requires that the dog win "legs" in ten shows. Utility Dogs who earn "legs" in Open B and Utility B earn points toward their Obedience Trial Champion title. In 1977 the title Obedience Trial Champion (OTCh.) was established by the AKC. To become an OTCh., a dog needs to earn 100 points, which requires three first places in Open B and Utility under three different judges.

The Grand Prix of obedience trials, the AKC National Obedience Invitational gives qualifying Utility Dogs the chance to win the newest and highest title: National Obedience Champion (NOC). Only the top 25 ranked obedience dogs, plus any dog ranked in the top 3 in its breed, are allowed to compete.

TRACKING

Any dog is capable of tracking, using his nose to follow a trail. Tracking tests are exciting and competitive ways to test your Doberman Pinscher's ability to search and rescue. The AKC started tracking tests in 1937, when the first AKC-licensed test took place as part of the Utility level at an obedience trial. Ten years later in 1947, the AKC offered the first title, Tracking Dog (TD). It was not until 1980 that the AKC added the Tracking Dog Excellent title (TDX), which was followed by the Versatile Surface Tracking title (VST) in 1995. The

MADISON SQUARE GARDEN CENTER
Seventh to Eighth Aves. & 31st to 33rd Streets, New York City
123rd ANNUAL DOG SHOW
THE WESTMINSTER KENNEL CLUB
MONDAY and TUESDAY, FEBRUARY 8 and 9, 1999
EXHIBITOR
NOT VALID UNLESS SIGNED
Nº
TUES. FEB. 9
Nº 2695
THE WESTMINSTER KENNEL CLUB
123rd ANNUAL DOG SHOW
MADISON SQUARE GARDEN CENT
EXHIBITOR
MON. FEB. 8
Nº 2695
THE WESTMINSTER KENNEL CLUB
Budweiser
TARGET
Coke
Budweiser
RING 4
RING 3
RING 2
WKC